Wings of a Firebird: The Power of Relationships in our Later Years

Concha Delgado Gaitan, Ph. D.

First Published in 2020 by Blossom Spring Publishing

Wings of a Firebird: The Power of Relationships in our Later Years

© 2020 Concha Delgado Gaitan

ISBN 978-1-8380188-8-7

E: admin@blossomspringpublishing.com

W: www.blossomspringpublishing.com

CONTENTS

In memory of an extraordinary storyteller in my life,
Angeles
Arrien, anthropologist, author, and speaker.
Thank you, my friend, for your wisdom about our later
years, which you taught with openness and love.

INTRODUCTION

Growing to become an older adult was not in my plans for much of my middle age life. No doctor expected me to live into my older years. Before my fortieth birthday I became quite disabled with a serious autoimmune illness that medical journals predicted only had a four percent recovery rate. When I asked doctors about my chances to get well, they responded with the same dismal news, "Most people like you with this condition just get weaker until the end." Mentally and spiritually I believed differently and rejected their negative prediction with every positive thought I could summon.

Through multiple traditional and alternative healing modalities, I grew stronger as birthdays passed. Around me, friends discussed their upcoming retirements. I couldn't picture what that would be for me. I appreciated being able to return to my career and enjoy my family and friends. These years were gifts. Beyond that, my future seemed nothing more than curiosity and mystery.

I wondered what older age would mean? What do older adults do? What would be important to me? Do people end up alone when they're older? How do people spend their life as older people? Who are the important people in their lives? What do people find meaningful to do in their older years? Many people talk about caring for their grandchildren, getting a hobby, volunteering, or starting different career. All of those things seemed important enough. What matters to me is remaining engaged in my research and writing profession working on social justice issues.

At the time that older age was a curiosity to me, my parents were nearing the end of their lives. I recalled that a few years prior they had grieved losing many family members and friends. I began thinking about the relationships that mattered to me and wondered which ones were most important to people as they aged. It's natural for me to write about people and communities, and I've learned a great deal from those life stories. Next to my family and social networks, my research work in Anthropology and Education has taught me that I'm intricately connected to the communities where I work.

Older people around me challenged me to understand not only about what aging means for me but about what relationships older adults across the country consider important. Reflecting on ways that relationships change over time raises questions about the expectations, dreams, and hopes for life we reach our later years. The snapshot of people's stories in this book, along with my reflections on aging portrays a cross-section of adults in various stages of aging. The people who shared stories here occupy work areas from housekeepers to professionals, and they reside in various regions of the country, working in distinct jobs and careers. A few were retired. They have different health aches and pains and different kinds of families. Socioeconomic conditions span from homeless to wealthy. Aging is the common denominator among the storytellers. Some are young seniors, others older adults.

Regardless of position on the senior continuum, the role of older adults in society is generally weaker because some policies isolate the group from the labor force, and because their incomes decline while the cost of living increases. During the senior years worry abounds about physical or mental illness. Through research and scientific studies on aging, gerontology informs us of the frequency of such problems during this period of life.

Parents, family members, neighbors, work colleagues, old and new friends share their stories in this book. They're not intended to illustrate role models of seniors in the category of health and caregiving, continuity and discontinuity of work, family cohesiveness and separation, grandparenting, reinvention of the oneself, and older adult activism and leadership. They're you and me. Readers may identify with the experiences in these life stories, or people in their lives may resemble seniors in the stories. These are stories without beginning or ending, making the message relevant in the present time.

Folk stories that lead into each chapter connect us to times past about elders and the themes in each chapter. When older adults survived difficult circumstances by finding ways to resolve conflict and discover their strength, they oftentimes rely on ancestral archetypes for dealing with their situations. These family oral folk traditions offered tradition, humor, and cleverness while reinforcing a group's identity. In this book, folk stories take us on roads of understanding and appreciating life's wisdom. Our cultural values can determine what knowledge means in the later years.

Communities where I've conducted anthropology and education research provided opportunities for me to collect oral traditions of families in diverse cultural communities. Many of the cultural groups include Hmong, Spanish, Russian Refugee, Mexican, El Salvadorian, and New Mexican households. Different family members tell stories to young children and sometimes to the entire family. Grandparents or older siblings tell stories to young children to instill a particular value or understand their family's history. Although mostly male family members tell the folk stories that appear here, the women play a leading role in those families with their children through story when they read books with them before bedtime.

In *Wings of a Firebird: The Power of Relationships in our Later Years* readers will recognize that for a myriad of reasons, some seniors have harder times than others in wrestling with life issues. However, an underestimated strength, creativity, and spirit that empower the diverse senior community to move forward inspires us. Throughout the life stories told here, I share how I'm embracing the surprises that I'm presented as I grow older and the lessons I learned from the many seniors whose lives enhanced this book. In part four, I tell my personal story with my father and coming to terms with my father as he reveals his true character. In the final reflection section, I conclude with commentary on how the present day global coronavirus pandemic has engrossed this country's attention on the need to provide more and better inclusive health services, safe housing, and economic resources for older adults across the United States.

I am deeply grateful to the people who have openly shared how relationships form their lives. In some cases, I restructured their narrative to order their stories in more chronological sequence. As well as being illuminating, their sharing of their situations and emotions compelled me to tell their stories. Learning of these relationships helps us to appreciate the value of staying engaged with family and friends. My hope is that these stories invite adult readers, including caregivers, to engage in conversation about the connections that matter. By humanizing the complex issues that the aging demographic faces, we're better able to anticipate and prepare our futures.

PART 1

RELATIONSHIPS IN CONTINUITY AND DISCONTINUITY

1

A NEW DAY

In a land far away, full of fresh ponds and surrounded by lush green trees, lived two young brothers, Adrian and Andre. In the castle on the highest hill, a king lived all alone, wishing he had a son. Adrian and Andre had many friends and were very popular. They loved competing with each other to see who could play the biggest prank on people and disturb their peace.

The king had always wanted a son to whom he could pass on the throne when his days were over. He had a contest for all of the young boys in his kingdom. He challenged them to bring him the worst criminal in the land. This was easy to do, you understand, because there were no prisons as we have here now.

The castle on the hill quickly filled with men that the boys felt should be prisoners. They were able to get them to come to the castle because the boys lied to them that the king would feed them a good meal. The two popular brothers now had competition.

The king welcomed all of the young boys and the criminals and gave them their most difficult part of this test, to show the goodness in the person they'd brought to the castle. The boys turned to one another and laughed, "That's impossible!" they yelled back to the king. "These are all bad men. Just feed us all and we'll leave."

"That's nonsense. Everyone has something good about them." The boys and the criminals again laughed.

Then, Andre walked forward to the king with the man he had brought to the castle. "Your majesty, I think this man I brought is a good person who did something bad."

The king asked him to explain what he meant. "I think this man stole money because he needed money to feed his family, your majesty. He's a good person because he tried to take care of his family."

"You're a smart young man, my son. And because you told me about this man's goodness, I will forgive his crime. And you, Andre, will live with me as my prince." Andre continued playing with all the boys in the land because the king allowed him to be playful with his brother and family. The king was now happy, and he wanted Andre to also be happy.

Niko's family invited many of his friends to his birthday celebration on a Sunday afternoon. After they enjoyed their delicious cake, Niko asked his father to tell them one of the king stories that they loved. All of Niko's friends liked hearing a happy ending to a story that began with a sad king. Niko's guests gathered around the table where his father regaled them with folk stories.

Niko's father showed that Andre relied on his sage knowledge to please the king. Niko realized that there was a different side to the criminal than most of the young men saw in the people they brought to the castle. Andre recognized a different way to relate to this stranger whom he'd once thought of as a felon.

Wisdom is the underpinning when there's something for us to solve as the king made the people in the kingdom understand that it was possible that people weren't all bad.

Life circumstances open opportunities for us to change our attitudes and beliefs about ourselves and others in our lives. A minor interference for some may feel like a major crisis for others, especially in the absence of supportive people to see us through rough patches in certain relationships.[1] With a support system of loved ones on our side, as older adults we're capable of looking within, rethinking attitudes and redirecting our lives. Anthropologist Angeles Arrien calls this seeing with an open heart.[2] Surprising ripples result when our mind and heart work together, thinking that better days might be behind us, then realizing that better days can also lie ahead.

Sofia, a former high school teacher, found herself in a new classroom with lessons she'd never expected to learn when her mother became too frail to care for herself. A senior herself, Sofia accepted her caregiving role for her 97-year-old mother Anita, through a terminal illness, though she had long experienced her mother as mean-spirited. Sofia moved into her mother's home, and for three years she learned about her mother's early life. Through day after day of cooking, helping to abate her mother's physical pain, and trying to make her life comfortable, Anita's revealing story would alter their relationship. Anita's early years' story became an unexpected gift.

"The mother I grew up with often seemed angry and unkind to my father. I didn't see a lot of affection between them when I was younger," Sofia said. "It was difficult to live in the midst of that relationship because I loved my dad very much. She always had a stern personality. When I cared for her, she revealed that her early years in El Paso were a terrible time.

They were very poor and had very little to eat and lived in ice-cold quarters resembling a warehouse. My uncles Manuel and Salvador were mean to each other and mean to the kids. For Mom, the past was palpable. She talked to me, trusting me like her best friend. Then she turned her face away from me and began to cry when she talked about how mean they were to her. I held her hand as I listened to her tell her story. 'I liked to do things like polishing the furniture, polish the floors, and ironing', she said. 'I could faint with all the ironing I had to do. I would mangle iron my father's work clothes. My cousins thought I was a slave to my mother, in some ways I was, but I didn't mind, I didn't mind. I liked to do the dirty work, but my mom would do things that were unkind. She would tell me that I had to do this and that when I wanted to go out with my friends to the park. She made me clean windows. If I protested, she'd hit me. I was unhappy doing all the cleaning because it was unfair. My brother, Sal was also mean. He did cruel things like torture my cat in front of me.'…"

Listening to Sofia, it seemed as though she was retelling a child's story in present time, not the life the life of an ailing elderly woman recalling ancient memories. This was partly true. Anita's fragile health left her vulnerable to unburdening herself of the painful days of her early life.

"Mom was six years old and the youngest one in her family. I needed to see and feel her place of origin for myself…I traveled to El Paso, and I photographed buildings. I brought them back for Mom. I knew she would love them. I showed her the place where she and her family lived according to the 1920 census. It was a warehouse with no windows. The place was a storefront on Texas Street in El Paso. The census said that six families were living back there behind the storefront."

Sofia wanted to understand how her mother Anita's early childhood had shaped Sofia's own early years. She decided she wanted to physically feel the geography of her mother's past. Her trip to El Paso, Texas led her to appreciate her mother's memories and to tell Anita's side of her story compassionately and honestly.

"Mom had suffered both at the hands of her mother and family as well as through the blatant discrimination on the part of white people in the town where they lived. Perhaps that contributed to shaping her personality. She was difficult to live with. Mom was very mean to us. She would say some things that always made me question why on earth such insulting things would be coming out of her mouth. I would ask her, Mom, why did you feel you had to say such things? She'd answer, 'I had to say that.' And again, I would tell her, No, you don't have to. Her unresolved pain carried into our family and the way in which she related to my father and her harsh ways with us. I'm grateful that she lived as long as she did and that I had the opportunity to care for her. It was very hard for me, but a part of me healed. The part of me that had become hardened softened. My empathy and appreciation grew for Mom for who she was, and I understood her ways.

Walking the same streets where Mom grew up convinced me that I was meant to care for my mother so I could move into my new stage of being a compassionate elder. I'm ready to help other women heal their inner wounds and discover joy in this vital stage of our lives."

In pursuing the pain that dominated Anita's life, Sofia unveiled a family history with the younger Anita as the victim, the opposite role she had played out as an adult. At the end of her life, Anita was able to change her bond with her daughter. Sofia had learned about Anita, and her new felt compassion softened her perception of her mother, thus humanizing their relationship. In so doing, Sofia healed her own inner child.

Sofia also recognized that in spite of it all, her mother had been the thread that held their family together. With time, patience, and love, relationship difficulties can reveal unexpected gems. In healing the inner child, concentration, energy, and insights improve, and lives transform.[3] After caring for her mother, Sofia felt compelled to share with others how to transcend pain and transform their relationships. She discovered her own wisdom as she moved into her elder status by mentoring young women.

Mercedes applied her wisdom differently. "I'm 95, and I love my life. How's that for a start?" Sitting in

Mercedes's home in a small, safe, suburban town near San Jose, California, it seemed as though I was stepping into my parents' home. Family photos of her three daughters and their families decorated every place the eye fell in the living room. Other family photos sat on the shelf counters below modern artwork hanging on the wall near the door.

When Mercedes opened the front door to her house, I saw a slight, five-foot tall woman with a ninety-five-year old warm smile. "Welcome," she said, "come in and sit down." She pointed to the long couch covered with a multicolor crochet throw.

Around her community, Mercedes's neighbors knew her as the fastest walker in town. Julia, one of her three daughters, lived a few blocks from her. She looked in on Mercedes daily. Except for transportation, Mercedes was quite self-sufficient. With the support of one of her daughters who lived nearby, she maintained her three-bedroom home, cooked for herself and volunteered in the local hospital at least once weekly.

Since surrendering her car keys two years before, Mercedes walked or got rides from Julia and other neighbors. Between family and friends around her, transportation was easy and convenient. But somehow I knew that her freedom didn't depend on public transportation. Her story, which began when Mercedes was a young girl emigrating from El Salvador with her mother, confirmed it.

She addresses an issue that plagues a significant part of society domestic violence. In the United States (US) nearly twenty-nine percent of women experience some form of abuse in their homes.[4]

"I lived with my mother in a tiny room in San Francisco and had little to eat. She had a job in a restaurant that paid a meager salary. I met a young man. He was my first boyfriend, and we got married right away.

He was older and was successful in his business. He worked hard, but he didn't let me work when we married. The arguments about me wanting to work increased. He would hit me when he found out that I had taken a job at a factory. The violence got worse after my daughters were born. If I went out with my friends or if I did not agree with him on something, he got very violent. Some arguments were about me wanting to work, and he didn't want me to leave the house to work. I was to keep a clean house and raise our three daughters.

I loved being with my girls, but I wanted a peaceful family for us all. My daughters were always very frightened when he hit me. He wasn't physically abusive to them. When they were old enough to drive, they would take me to the emergency room to stitch-up my bloody head. Many times during the marriage, I found myself at the emergency room with a cracked skull in need of stitches. Each time I returned I made sure he knew that I was not going to quit my work at the coffee factory.

As the girls grew up, my oldest daughter began standing up to him. And she kept insisting that I leave him. When the girls were grown up, they tried to help me separate from their father, but he always convinced me to return. When they began their independent lives, they stayed close to me as much as they could to keep me safe.

They've always been such loving daughters. Their adoring presence and their hugs and kisses got me through many painful times."

Mercedes related the events in a matter of fact way until she talked about the loving support that her daughters had always given her. Her voice quivered a bit, and she glanced at their photos on the tables near the couch where she sat with tear-filled eyes.

"My girls cared for me since they were young adults. They protected me, and I believe that's how I'm still alive. After my daughters left the house, I continued working and slowly found my power to leave my husband. I filed for divorce. This time I refused to reconcile.

My divorce was long overdue. When I finally found myself divorced, it was like the clouds parted, and I saw God! My husband like always in the past wanted us to get back together, but no more. My daughters made sure of that. I would never keep them from having contact with him. He was their father. After the divorce, the girls visited him. Even I communicated with him sometimes."

When speaking about her divorce, Mercedes' head lowered, and her voice dropped. A silent pause marked the end of a struggle-filled part of her story.

"I was close to seventy and had retired from work at the coffee company, but I was eager to return to work. That's where I was happy, so I returned. Three years after

I returned, the coffee company forced me to retire. They wanted to hire younger people who could work the assembly line faster. They brought in new equipment, and they didn't want to spend time training me. When I stopped working, I found lots of things to do on my own, things I couldn't do when I worked and raised my daughters. At first, I was sad because I loved my work, but then I found so many other things I enjoyed doing.

The girls continued to visit my ex-husband, and they cared for him until he remarried. I was glad that he remarried because he had someone to take care of him." Mercedes emphasized that she even liked the woman he married. "My ex-husband brought his wife to meet me. I liked her. She was a lovely person. We became friends when she opened up to me about her frustration because he refused to allow her to learn to drive. He expected her to stay home. I gave her my strong opinion about that part of marriage."

Mercedes encouraged the woman to assert herself and learn to drive on her own. She told her to stop depending on her husband to liberate herself. Mercedes was happy to help her former husband's new wife to liberate herself. She had spent too many years of her own life in terror to turn a deaf ear to her.

"A few years after the divorce, my ex-husband became very ill with cancer. My daughters helped him and his wife during the illness. I supported all of the women to care for him until he died.

I'm extremely fortunate to have survived my violent past and to have reached ninety-five. Since my divorce, it's been the time of my life. I'm free. I don't forget my violent past, but I don't want to keep torturing myself. I've forgiven my ex-husband. It's over. He's gone, and so is everything that happened during that period of my life. I stay healthy thanks to my daughters who care for me. I do Yoga and Zumba dance classes, which my daughter Julia teaches at the community center. I volunteer weekly at the local hospital."

In Mercedes' earlier years, she experienced the harm that many women face. In the US, a woman is physically abused by an intimate partner every nine seconds.[5] Throughout her marriage, Mercedes refused to report the domestic violence and press charges. She bypassed the entanglements of law enforcement, lawyers, courts, and other social services where many battered women who find themselves. Mercedes, like many women who remain in violent relationships, found ways to accommodate and survive the abuse within the marriage.[6] She was very fortunate to have survived the abuse. From a cultural perspective, some women like Mercedes who find themselves in domestic violence situations prefer to address family problems somewhat privately.[7] The role of women in some traditional cultures determines the subjugation of women to men. With such power relations in place, Mercedes' decision to end her marriage shows the strength she had built up to liberate herself.

Without Mercedes analysis of her reason for befriending her former husband's new wife, I speculated that her act represented Mercedes' own path to transforming her former relationships. She put her injurious relationship with her ex-husband in the past by sharing with her former husband's wife the experience that she had not practiced herself. By so doing, she claimed her strength.[8]

Throughout her home, Mercedes displays her heartfelt freedom in thriving plants, in the colorful rooms, and the bright crochet throws on couches. In one wall-hanging picture of herself, she flaunted her sense of freedom. In an 8x10 picture frame, Mercedes had cut out the figure of a magazine model in a bathing suit and replaced the head with a present-day picture of her own face. She had scissored out words from the magazine, put them together, and pasted them next to the model. They read, "Mercedes ran out of money when she got to her face." It was this humor and wisdom that saved her from the inevitable fate that many women encounter every day.

For Len, reaching his later years was an introspective period. "There was a time when I was ready to collapse into old age, maybe a few years ago. I ached too much, and I don't watch television, so I got depressed and went down the chute. I was lying in bed, and I imagined an endless escalator going down, and I got to the bottom, and there I was on solid ground. I dug myself out of some profound grief, and I took what I have, and I'm still doing it, making myself as whole as I can be."

In his eighth decade, Len searched and found the lenses he needed to understand his life obstacles in a different way than he had dealt with them in earlier years.

As his spirituality lightened his toughest difficulties. Len appreciated the possibilities for the quality of his life.

"I'm 87 now, and I was in my early 80's then, and overweight and I had aches and pains. I had an excellent session with my doctor who advised me to read Eric Erickson, a German psychoanalyst about old age. Of course, in my readings I thought about the whole matter of being old. So, I did come up with a sense that it's okay. I can go there. I realized that I was depressed, and I could admit it. I learned that it was chemical and triggered by the problem of PTSD, which I have. Most of the time PTSD people go into cognitive therapy, but you don't relive the trauma that way. The last time I went to visit my psychiatrist I said, 'I'm sad about the loss of my friend.' I told him that I was despondent, but I didn't want medication. He said, 'good for you. Just feel it. Grief is an appropriate feeling. We have to express it.'

I have an excellent psychiatrist that helped me gain some insights. Did I feel I was getting old? Yes, for a moment. I know that older age means losing more dear ones. Now, all I have is a body and it's getting older and older, but I feel my mind and my spirit are fully awake—more than ever. Sure, my memory roams more and more, but it's free to roam. It's not like senility at all. I'm not senile, but it's freedom from words-very Zen. It is very Buddhist. I don't believe I'm enlightened, but then who the hell knows what that is."

I chuckled with Len when he realized that enlightenment is an illusion. He returned to his explanation, quoting the Buddha.

"Enlightenment is not like violins playing. The Buddha said you've got to come down from the mountain, meaning that we have to put our thoughts into action. I believe another thing he said was life is suffering. And that's what we make peace with—the real world.

I suffer for this country. I feel that in some way, we have disappointed the whole world and ourselves. We're not as old as Europe, and it's decayed. A hundred years ago, Tocqueville predicted that democracy would happen gradually. He loved justice and freedom. He predicted that's what would happen is that society would be taken up by uneducated people willing to push. I'm paraphrasing it. Where the state will eventually become an oligarchy ruled by the provocation and manipulation of the mass public and in that way, democracy becomes a weapon in the hands of oligarchs. I see that happening, and the suffering in this world is unbelievable. I mean I feel the suffering because of my Jewish background, my time in Dachau, which I have tried to confront throughout my life because of my PTSD and living with a mother that I don't think ever left there. I know atrocities like those still go on in the world, and I can do little about it. I used to think I could when I was younger, but now I'm lost about how to change these atrocities.

What does an eighty-seven year-old person who has trouble walking do about it? I sign petitions, I send money, and I hold on to the universe. It's not a solution, but I have to place myself in the real world. On the other hand, Buddha was most concerned with people's suffering. That's been mine as well. I've been doing that all my life, I've walked in marches, I've picketed the White House against the bomb when Eisenhower was in office. I'm getting old, but I still care.

People of any age can be elders, but it's usually older people who impart their wisdom. Elder is wisdom. We've all known younger adults who have wisdom. However, elders are the ones who really can understand. Unfortunately, the society puts elders, old people, in very, comfortable jails, and they seek it. They find homes where they can all gather together, eat together, play bridge, be comfortable, and relax into their comfort. That's something I dread. I will not go. I want to die here, preferably out here in the garden, like the Godfather. There's another great poem, it begins, 'the world is too much with me.' And that's true the world is too much with us and one feels helpless, but then that's how we're born, helpless. We are dependent and we bond together trying to be helpful. Look at the poor-they have bonded. The American people have done horrible things to the African-Americans and Native Americans, and Latinos as we all know. We've broken those bonds that they have had with each other. We have done the utmost to break up the indigenous and slave families. It's evil, pure evil. It's the elders that are holding those communities together, barely by being strong. That's strength. That's an elder.

A memorable example is when I worked in Holland for a couple of years, teaching in a school for schizophrenic kids. They weren't schizophrenic. They were just disturbed kids. There were forceful women working in those communities. The management didn't prepare the young women to do what was expected of them, which was horrifically difficult work. All of those young women failed and left. The older women were hanging in there, caring for everyone because of their belief in a grand primitive Christianity-'eldering.'"

Len spoke of eldering, that stage of life that helps us draw on life's experience to nurture, heal, and reach out to younger generations, encouraging them to appreciate their gifts and to give back to care for communities. The multi-faith Spiritual Eldering Institute embraces the idea that in later life older adults can reframe past hurts that result in deep creativity and wisdom.

"My daughter lives the values of caring for the others and the planet. I hope this is the legacy my grandson appreciates. Wisdom is action in senior years as depicted in the book *From Age-ing to Sage-ing.*[9] Being old, I guess I'm finally feeling a sense of grace."

Through multi-faith lenses, Len positions himself as an elder, appreciating the wisdom of his life. His wife, daughter, grandson, and an active group of friends have contributed to shaping his life. They've supported him in maintaining a calm attitude, to peacefully accepting being alive and awakening in his elder stage. He transformed his resentments and obstructions to feeling his real character. Through it all, he discovered his authentic self and his courage.

Change was a long time coming for Karla. "I'm retiring soon, and I've been feeling restless about my big and not so big life stressors. Reviewing the big picture of my life, I had to go back to my school days, not because of school but how I managed to get through it.

When my younger sister and brother were in the eighth grade, I took our mother to the psychiatric hospital, where she spent many years. I was in high school then. We didn't tell anyone about the situation because the authorities would separate us. I took care of them while I finished high school and got myself into college with a scholarship. Creative financing methods and food pantries in the area kept us going. I helped my brother and sister through high school and made sure that we all had jobs that brought in a meager income."

The strength she sought was not of physical endurance. She wished for inner harmony. Karla welcomed her renewal as a senior with a deliberate and strong intention to minimize stress in life. She was tired of struggling through her life's tribulations. Looking deep within, she wanted more calm and joy. With inner calm she expected to feel more enjoyment.

Karla felt that the healthy way to minimize the daily tensions that she had lived with most of her life meant finding balance. Identifying the strength to make sense of the world doesn't always come from a single person laying the foundation in the early years. Sometimes it means remaining open to insights from people who may speak that truth we're ready to hear. Listening inspires us to find the comfort zone from where we act.

"When I cared for my younger siblings, family members knew about the situation, but they rarely visited. They didn't offer much. We missed my mother because when she was well, she was a real firecracker—singing and dancing. The house was full of life. She taught us songs, dances, and other arts. To this day, I appreciate my gifts for painting and sculpting. Mom taught us all that.

By the time I got into law school, my mother was home, and my siblings had their own lives. I was glad not be to be raising siblings and an ill mother. I was able to leave home and strike out on what became my career. Not only did I work as a lawyer, but I also taught at Berkeley Law School. When I married, I couldn't imagine having children. I'd already done my work. As a lawyer I worked in family law, which I enjoyed a great deal. In addition to law school, my early years prepared me well for working in this area of law."

I quietly took a deep breath at this point. The background story of her early years had felt like a steam train rolling out of control. It had already shown me how events in her family had made her an adult who'd enormous responsibilities in her early years. With another deep breath, I prepared for more of her story.

"For too many years, I remember enjoying my work but feeling mostly stress while working and doing life. But one thing that I've always felt close to was my spirituality and positive attitude. In my quiet time, I have meditations and readings that I rely on for inspiration. Yet for some time, I felt less able to connect with that peace."

Karla committed herself to her work in the courts as a staff attorney representing legal cases of families when custodial issues were in conflict. This was demanding work itself in the amount of negotiation required. Additionally, an emotionally traumatic veil characterized the families' case. Her cases often involved grandparents and other family members who fought to have control of the children after a family tragedy when the parents could no longer do it.

In one situation, a couple had a four-year-old daughter. They lived in a small apartment and seemed friendly and social with their neighbors. One day, the grandmother called on the apartment manager when she came to visit. The couple didn't answer as they always did on weekends. When she walked in, her granddaughter sat, stoical, saturated in blood between her two parents, who had been shot. The mother was barely alive and gave the police a couple of leads before she died. Without any instructions of where the child should go in case of such emergencies, the grandmother took her grandchild and held on to her tight as she feared what might happen to the child. She loved her grandchild and knew her daily routine. She thus felt that she would make the best custodian for granddaughter. Just prior to the family court deciding this case, which Karla presented, a maternal aunt and uncle appeared in court with a competing application. They felt that they should be awarded the orphan child because they had a daughter about the same age.

Regularly Karla mediated these conflicts in court. Although she liked her work and was quite effective in resolving the daily conflicts that ensued, the pressure undermined her health. Even her loving family life and artwork did not buffer the stress in her life. Karla describes how she transformed her life from the high-strung pace she lived to one more relaxed and calmer.

"I returned to my favorite prayer. It's simple - about a little priest who has been deceased for about ten or twelve years. He used to start his service with, 'there are many ways to the creator minus but one.' That's when I really started listening and paying attention to what that really meant. The prayer is a kind of self-exploration. But the fact that it's the context that there are many ways to the creator minus 'but one' is like saying my struggle is my struggle. While that's true, other people struggled too. It just came cloaked this way, and the way I didn't even have to struggle, but I have, my spiritually.

I heard Angela Davis speak on PBS. Something

she said impressed me. She said that struggle gives her hope. And I understand how she's motivated that way and that her philosophy drives her, but part of me says I don't want to struggle anymore. I really don't want to struggle anymore."

Karla's declaration mirrored a time in my own history when I had felt a need for major life changes. I admired her honesty in examining her need for a different vision.

"Even working for social justice should not be a struggle. Everybody's path is to be dignified and respected as his or hers. To me, that kind of takes out part of the struggle, if I accept you then I accept you as well as me. But in my work as an attorney in the courts there's only one way I could have dealt with one particular case that landed on my lap. I cared about him and the case, so I realized this is why I asked him, 'What the hell are you doing?' I don't want to get into the details of the case now, but suffice it to say that I had a strong feeling that the man wasn't being honest and for me to represent him, he needed to know that I was on his side. But I too had to be honest with myself and not allow him to walk all over me. Whatever he decided was up to him, but I didn't want to struggle with him. I wanted to convince him to be other than whom he was projecting. I got a chance to observe and support him in his issues that mattered, but I had to change my relationship to him. And now there's just a lot of richness in our relationship because I'm lucky enough to recognize the depth of someone else's pain while recognizing that I'm not there to solve their problems-only to support them in their defense. I've distinguished my role as family law lawyer from my early childhood years in solving family crisis."

Karla then talked about Joe Dispenza, a New York Times bestselling author, researcher, chiropractor and lecturer. "He taught neuroscience and human potential to thousands of people around the world. I appreciate that he empowers one with the knowledge and tools to conquer destructive and everyday habits so that we can reach our vision and goals. His approach bridges the gap between neuroscience and true human potential. He explains how you can literally rewire your brain to create a new mind and produce new results in your life. For me, he helped me connect my body and spirit. And that was a link that wasn't that clear to me before. Dispenza literally tells us that all of the body's nerve centers are arranged in a way that connects to the brain. This created a real spiritual experience for me. I feel that the potential is so great. I can see glimpses of his work in me-how can I not be in love with this world, with this beautiful earth? I feel that connection with all that's good even more now. The awareness of feeling connection that I've learned through this relationship with Joe because he gives me a certain depth. I definitely feel more depth. I look at the clouds and I'm more connected with clouds. It's kind of cool. It allows me to be more child-like, to have a relationship with my inner child. I could never do that when I maintained a wildly hectic routine. Who has time to look at clouds with an impossibly hectic calendar? When I felt the need to be so busy, everything felt like a struggle.[10]

My relationships with colleagues changed for the better. I told the judge yesterday, 'I'm not going to see you for a while,' and he hugged me. I was wearing red and spring green and, he said, 'Who dressed you today, Karla your inner child?' I just laughed. I feel more child-like."

Our cultural beliefs make our daily lives easier. Beliefs are familiar, and they work for us. Somewhere during childhood, we made decisions, then spent the rest of our lives convinced by those beliefs and live our lives accordingly.

Changing our thinking, beliefs and practices is not always a conscious process. However, inner pain makes it necessary for people to consciously review their life patterns and accept new perspectives. Karla's spirituality helped to release her from the stressful routine that had controlled her life since her early years. She felt that her career accomplishments had come with a high price tag. Her frenzied professional schedule her prevented her from resolving personal and work related problems which she'd overlooked. Karla became unwilling to continue paying the price and removed her blindfolds.

Most of us tenaciously hold onto our values whether they're expressed consciously or used as guideposts. Often, we move about life's daily routines and long-term plans without a second thought. Not everyone is interested in consciously changing their mind or attitudes about their life as did Karla. She wanted to live her life differently.

Wisdom unfolds uniquely different in the lives of Karla, Sofia, Mercedes, and Len. The traumas in their stories reveal the devastation of some primary relationships from their earlier years which they reverse in their later years. As living organisms, we're integrally connected to one another, making the interactions of all things matter at any given moment. With discernment and with family and community support, toxic relationships can be transformed into new and healthier ones.

2

WITH COMPASSION

An older couple lived outside a small quiet small town near the capital, San Salvador. It was a friendly place where everyone knew one another, and they were kind to each other. They didn't have children, but everyone called them Grandma and Grandpa. A young couple, the Calvos, lived on a farm and Grandma and Grandpa Solis cared for their chickens and goats along with the few crops they grew. They took the eggs and vegetables to the town farmers' market every Saturday morning. The town's people loved the food they sold because Grandma and Grandpa Solis kept the farm animals happy and they grew very healthy crops.

One day Mr. Solis became ill and Mrs. Solis told him to rest in bed and she would care for the animals and the crops. She kept her promise. Day after day, she fed the animals and cleaned the vegetable gardens until she got so exhausted caring for the farm by herself that she couldn't continue. The Solis couple could not afford his medicine. Grandma Solis asked the pharmacy to give them the medicine on credit. The pharmacist said, "No." When the town's people heard about this, they took their business to another pharmacy.

Grandma then asked Mr. and Mrs. Calvo to help her and her husband. They said that they would not help because it wasn't their responsibility. The people in town heard about the Solis's problem with the Calvos, and they stopped buying eggs from the Calvos at the farmer's market.

The Calvos told the Solis couple to find another home. The Calvo farm became unkempt and the chickens did not lay eggs. Very soon after leaving the Calvo farm, Grandpa and Grandma found a home to live where the owners were kind. They helped the Solises until they got well.

The Ortiz children enjoyed this story about the Solis family because they loved their grandparents, and the ending to the story showed that the older couple had many friends who cared for them. They liked that the Solis grandfather got well and found a home and work on another farm. In the Ortiz home, the grandfather and grandmother lived with their son's family including the three young children. Grandfather walked the children home after school. The children quickly did their homework, so they'd have time to hear a story from Grandfather before dinner.

Who will care for me when my health wanes? Who can I call to take me to the doctor? To speak of caregiving is to speak of relationships. When health needs take priority, who will step up to be with us? Answering these questions is simpler for some than for others. How those relationships play out can mean drama or joy or both during the caregiving period.

Caring for senior adults in their home, or anywhere else including a care facility, often means preparing their clothes, making sure they take their medications, feeding them, and in some cases assisting them to their end. Emotional closeness occurs as trust builds between the caregiver and the elder and they find ways of communicating about care needs.

When the caretaking is long and arduous, involving enormous responsibility, the caretaker's health may also become compromised. The physical toll of caretaking on caregivers has been studied enough for us to appreciate. Emotional stamina is foremost for the caretaker.[1]

At any age, we may find ourselves caretaking for someone close to us. Healthy relationships vary from a simple act of kindness such as saying good morning to the same person every day to having a cup of tea with friends who have similar interests as your elderly parent.

A concern that elders frequently spoke about was having someone in their lives upon whom they could count on for support in dealing with their health. Those who may not have had severe health problems were caregivers of people close to them. In this day and age, life extends longer than before. Given that fact, the worry about who will care for us haunts us more than ever in this country. For many, the salient concern, in addition to the question of having enough money to care for our medical problems, is who will care for us.

As ceasing work in later years occurs for many reasons, many people spoke with me about the plans and questions they had before retiring. Will there be enough money for me to live on after retirement? Many raised the inevitable concern, Am I financially secure enough to retire? Do I have good healthcare coverage? What if I need special care?

Those who counted on their work to define a great deal of their days asked themselves, Am I ready for retirement? Among their worries are having a is the social network once they leave their workplace and loss of friends and family as they age. Choices and concerns for senior adults about what happens after retirement bewilder some retirees, but not Jean. She looked forward to retiring from her legal secretarial position in a Denver, Colorado firm.

Jean and I talked three years after she had celebrated her retirement and accomplishments with a festive dinner at her favorite restaurant in Denver surrounded by her friends. Not only had Jean celebrated her "big 60" as she called it, but that night she surprised everyone with the news that she was retiring from thirty years at her secretarial position in a small law firm. Her forty-five-minute commute to Denver in heavy traffic would be in the past. "I'll be sleeping in till at least 7:00 A.M," Jean announced to her friends, "Then it's out the door to run, have coffee with friends and stay current with the morning paper. That should last at least a week or two until I get itchy and begin thinking about my next job. Up to now, I've been too busy to plan anything." Jean crossed the border from her fifth to her sixth decade excited and prepared to simplify her life.

Following her retirement, Jean's decisions were as much a surprise to her as they were to her family and friends because prior to retirement, she had made her life outside of Denver. Her social life had centered on volunteering at a women's shelter and serving on the board of the scholarship foundation for underprivileged students, along with the church where she'd worshiped for years. In this community, Jean had married, and she and her husband had raised their daughter and son. They enjoyed traveling to destinations around the US, and a couple of times they made trips to other countries. They especially liked camping and visits to Italy and Mexico City.

Most of the time Jean enjoyed her work. For a couple of years, she cut back from a full-time job to part-time in the office and took home some unfinished work. Caring for her husband took priority and consumed much of her time. Tom had developed kidney cancer and needed multiple treatments along with a great deal of care at home. When her daughter and son completed college, they each moved to North Carolina for work. There they married and had children, making infrequent visits to Colorado. Jean saw her family every other year at Christmas, and they Skyped weekly during the year. When their father became ill, the grown daughter and son visited more often. All the family was with him during his last hospitalization.

After her husband died, Jean thought that it might be time for her to do some things besides work. She looked forward to leisure time. She welcomed the anticipated changes from full-time work to more time for friends and volunteering.

But along with retirement, another change came rapidly for Jean.[2]A few months after retiring she fell while on her morning run, route that was a familiar path for her. She had fallen before, but this time she felt shaky and unable to balance herself. Her hip had hit the concrete harder than other times. After several days, she still felt too sore to run, and she made an appointment to visit her doctor. Jean had test after test, but results showed only bruising on her hip. She was advised to refrain from running for a while and do a gentle workout instead. A specialist she consulted with referred her to a neurologist. Jean was not alarmed. She, however, felt annoyed that her stiff body and many tests interfered with her three to five-mile morning run. Running would have to wait for a while. She filled her day with friends at lunch and worked at the women's shelter as often as she could.

"The specialist called me and asked to see me in his office to discuss the imaging results. I went to the appointment by myself because I never imagined that he would report anything but the ordinary bruising, maybe suggest that I walk, instead of run, for a while. The news couldn't have been more shocking. He said they found that I had early stages of Parkinson's disease."

Stunned, Jean sat alone without anyone to comfort her. "I was so horrified I couldn't even cry. Where was someone to hug me? I felt so cold and alone from the shock. I was angry, first that I had the disease, but at that moment I hated the specialist for not warning me to have a friend accompany me. I collected myself and went home. I wanted to call Tom, then I realized he couldn't help me, wherever he was. I wondered whom else I might call, but that didn't feel right. I didn't want to tell my kids over the phone. Not right now. My mind was everywhere and nowhere. Part of me wanted to go running to show my body that it was wrong. Maybe the specialist was wrong. Maybe I didn't have Parkinson's. I'll get another opinion. How is it possible that I could I end up with this crippling disease? I'm active and fit."

Up to the time that she talked about hearing her diagnosis, Jean's held herself together emotionally as she had done through caring for her husband and maintaining her career. She described to me what she did with her angry emotions aimed at the doctors and how she let herself feel the full impact of the distressing news. She spoke slowly during our talk, and throughout the interview, her voice held up with only an occasional pause. When she told me about meeting with her son and daughter I listened as she said how her daughter hugged her in tears while her son sat quietly. They talked with her about ways to simplify her living for a while and then consider moving to be with the daughter.

Time became Jean's friend and enemy. On the one hand, she was in the early stages of the disease. The doctor told her that if she maintained a good exercise routine daily, a healthy diet along with prescribed physical therapy and substantial sleep, she could reduce the progression of the disease. At home, she began making precautionary changes around the house to assist her as the Parkinson's progressed. She lowered kitchen cupboards enabling her to store supplies at a reasonable reach without a stepladder, and she kept a list of helpers next to her phone for her needs like shopping or household chores.

On the other hand, she was advised to stop her morning runs and walk only with a companion. She slowed to a fast walk while she underwent more tests. She knew not to push it to where she might fall again and further impair her mobility. Spending time with friends became a daily ritual. Finding an attendant to drive her around and assist around the house was her next step.

Jean said, "When I first retired, I thought that I might want to pursue a new career, and I still want to do that. Not sure of the nature of the work I want to do, but I know I want to do something meaningful. That gives me hope.

So, this is retirement. When he was alive, neither Tom nor I pictured retirement in a rocking chair in these later years. For sure, I didn't see myself in a wheelchair, alone without my husband and my children across the country. I still don't. I don't want to stop my life because of this diagnosis, but I do feel more fatigued during the day. I'm not used to feeling tired. I'm usually very energetic. Maybe, as they say, this is the 'new normal.' I'm still planning to travel to North Carolina to visit my grandchildren and spend as much time with them as possible. I don't see myself moving east as my kids suggest because I love Colorado. I have major decisions to make about who will care for me in the long run. Will it be an assisted care facility? Hire someone to assist me at home so I can continue living here? Maybe. My friends are great, but they can't do full-time assistance for me. I'm sure my son and daughter will expect to come out and help me when the time comes, but Colorado is my home. It's all fairly new to me. I'm living in a surreal world. I've shed plenty of tears - alone. I miss Tom a lot these days. Sometimes I call on my friends and ask them to just listen. But, at the same time, I feel that it's a blessing that they caught it early."

Simplifying her life after retirement took a very different turn for Jean as her health forced her into a new plan. It would all become more complicated than she ever imagined. With the help of her family and friends, Jean moved forward with strong optimism as she discovered different ways of living and a new meaning for her life from what she'd hoped when she first retired.

With a few states between them, Jean's son and daughter couldn't assist her in her daily caregiving. Finding oneself alone during a health crisis in later years is familiar to many single people. Married women outlive men or are divorced by their senior years, making them more vulnerable when a health crisis arises.

Jean's situation resembles that of many families who have dispersed as a result of young people leaving for college or work. Family members pursue different interests and preferences of places to live. As we age, loss of people and things becomes more common, including loss of good health along with a career, as in Jean's case. Some research reveals that social networks tend to reduce in size as compared to the younger adult period, although the quality of some relationships deepens in later-year relationships.[3] A loss, however, can awaken us to new experiences.

Single adults often remark, "I don't have a partner. I don't have children. My friends have as many health issues as I have. A cousin lives several states away, so if something happens to me, I don't know what I'll do because I don't have the money to pay live-in help." It's easy to concern ourselves with the question of who would care for us when we're not in the midst of the crisis. Often, when we're in the midst of a situation a helping hand appears in unexpected ways. Wondering who will care for us concerned many people I interviewed unless they lived in a family where culturally defined roles take precedence.

Lulu, a twenty-five-year old Filipina young woman, left her hometown. Her elderly mother, Gloria, stayed behind. "Mom was sad to watch me leave, but she said, 'Lulu, I pray this move makes your dreams come true. You work hard. We'll see each other often.' She knew I would have many more opportunities for nursing in Nevada than in the Philippines."

Lulu feared leaving her mother behind in Tagaytay, Philippines when she moved to Clark County, Nevada. But Lulu, as her family called her, left with her head held high. She looked forward the challenge of nursing school and living near her extended family. Although Lulu was her mother's primary caretaker, she felt confident that Gloria would be fine since she was healthy.

When Lulu left, Gloria continued living in the home where her daughter had grown up. Within months after Lulu's departure, her mother had a heart attack. With existing diabetes and other complications, Gloria needed a great deal of help to recover. Caregiving roles are often relegated to women, more so in traditional cultures that immigrate to the US. Lulu stepped up to her role as expected and returned home for a short stay to help her mother. Lulu, however had to return to Nevada to her studies and her work.

"As Mom's health weakened, I knew my responsibilities would increase. Our culture makes it clear. When I left Tagaytay, I knew that I wasn't leaving Mom. I'll always want to care for her. At the time, I didn't have it all worked out in my head, but I knew that it would involve lots of traveling when I moved to Nevada and I was willing to do it. She's my mother, and I'll always care for her. Caring for our elders is the family's responsibility. I just didn't think Mom would need me to help her so much now. Mom's relatives work and visit her often, but every day she seemed to need more daily help."

In my own family, our maternal grandparents lived with us during our earlier years. Their health always seemed to be a particular concern, so when they were quite old, and they became frailer, their health seemed to be part of this daily care for each other.[4] In many cultures, living and caring for each other in an extended family involves every member, including the young grandchildren. To break from one's culture of origin can be a difficult adjustment for someone older.

The absence of a residential senior care facility in the Philippines town where Lulu's mother lived meant major decisions, not only for Gloria but for her own mother and other family members. Although Lulu's mother needed assisted living care, her preference was to live with her family, a decision rooted in her cultural values. This forced Lulu to reassess her priorities.

"Other family members who live in the Philippines are older and have their health problems. I wish she'd come and live with me, but she loves

Tagaytay, it's her home. I love it too. It's beautiful, but there aren't opportunities for me to develop professionally in my nursing. Now, I have a job as an LVN while I finish my RN program and long flights to the Philippines have become my study hall in the air.

My heart ached every time I visited because she tells me that she's lonely. And I can't help her with that. For over a year, I Skyped from Nevada at least once a week. But of course, that wasn't enough. She was concerned about me being out here without her, but I felt that she was telling me that she was afraid of living alone. My brother talks to her too, but she needs so much more. She cooks very little, but when she does cook, she tells me in Tagalong, 'Lulu, I made lots of pancit. I know how you love it, but I forgot that I was alone.' I was familiar with my mother's legendary guilt trips, and she thought that making more pancit then she could ever eat by herself would tug at my heartstrings. I love my mother. I expect to care for her as long as she needs me. I wish she knew that she didn't have to use her tricks to get my attention.

After Mom began heart problems, I hired a woman to come in and fix her meals, but my mother needs so much more during the day. I'd made all of the arrangements for the women to take care of Mom and they get settled in the house, it's no problem hiring. Many people need work. They were comfortable being there. The problem is that they leave any job quickly because they have family conflicts of their own and can't continue. I tried to settle the issue on Skype, but at some point, I had to make that painfully long trip."

Lulu had lived alone while attending college and a nursing program in Nevada. Her cousins lived nearby. They were quick to support each other. However, caring for her ailing mom later on fell on Lulu's shoulders without warning. She didn't anticipate the challenges and lessons that awaited her. Her mother became increasingly weaker after her heart complications. Straddling her work and caring for her mother, Lulu said, "I began to feel overwhelmed."

Lulu's brother lives in Nevada outside of Clark County, and his family and obligations prevent him from visiting their mother more often. Lulu became the primary caregiver. She stays a few days to do everything her mother needs to be as comfortable as possible, but one thing Lulu cannot do for her mother: stop her loneliness.

Gloria's health circumstances and Lulu's increasing responsibilities caused Lulu to reassess her life plan. One year after settling in Nevada, she realized that her mother couldn't continue living so far away from her. While Skyping with her mother one day, Lulu felt it was time to force her to take an important step. Gloria moved to Nevada to live with her daughter. "I didn't know how it would work, but my brother and I talked to our cousins about how possible it would be to bring Mom to live with us. After everything I'd been through caring for her from so far away, any other way had to be better."

Lulu's brave solution impressed me. Her loyalty to her family and her embrace of her responsibility to care for her mother while pursuing her education and career showed a great deal of maturity. In our conversations, her warmth and her calm voice set a relaxed tone. Lulu said that she had counted on her family to assist with her mother's transfer to the US. She placed a good deal of trust in her extended family to support her in the plan that would follow for her mother's care. Their family system, however, differed somewhat from the traditional way in which Filipino older adults spend their later years.[5]

Gloria didn't hesitate when Lulu and her brother proposed their plan to move her to Nevada. Her brother hoped that possibly once she was living with them, he'd be able to assist more with her care. Lulu requested a leave of absence from her job and nursing school to make legal and household arrangements. Gloria's move to the US forced family members to reassess their priorities in relations to visiting her now that she lived nearer.

Gloria's values clashed with what she perceived were those of the new country, where her family now lived. She based her fear on the reputation that the US has for relegating seniors to lesser social and economic ranks. Lulu and her brother assured Gloria that living in a new country had not changed their family's values about caring for their mother. After their conversation, Lulu developed a new interest in attending a senior day center where some Filipino elders attended.

Moving from one region of the country to another or to a new culture forces people to adjust to different climates, languages, new relationships, and new places of worship. All of these changes magnify emotional response when seniors are forced to move to be near loved ones for healthcare. In a new culture with different values, Gloria feared that her health would decline and that she would end up in a senior care facility.

Gloria loved her family and wanted to be near them, but Lulu reminded her that the family had not lived with her reliably in Tagaytay. When Lulu lived with her there, Gloria had been healthy and able to care for Lulu while she went to school. Lulu's brother and family had lived in the US many years. Gloria expected her family to gather often when she reunited with them in Nevada. Now in Lulu's home, she feared the worst—to be left alone if her health became too much trouble for her family.

"Oh, the changes that we experienced to make life easier. At first, I loved having Mom in my home. We were together and she hugged me a lot like she used to when I lived with her in Tagaytay. But my mother didn't take well to the cold winter weather and dry, hot summer. I wasn't home during the day, so she was alone and felt lonely. As often as possible my sister-in-law and the grandchildren came, and cousins visited and brought food. I prepared meals so Mom could heat them during the day. I could tell, however, that she was missing her home. Finally, one day she confessed that she liked living with me and seeing my brother and her grandchildren who lived nearby, but she felt afraid that this country didn't value old people much. Her comment confused me. I asked her what she meant. Was there something that needed to be done for her? I admit to feeling a bit frustrated because I didn't know what more to do to satisfy her and I was falling behind in my studying at night because I shopped, cooked, and washed laundry. Mom helped in whatever way she could, but I did most of the work. Then she shocked me. She was afraid we'd put her in a senior home if she became too much work for us. She couldn't bear to lose her family."

Different weather, different home, new medical doctors, different daily routine, and an unfamiliar language distressed Gloria as she adjusted living with her family. Lulu discussed the problem with her brother and cousins, asking for ideas about how to make Gloria more comfortable. The cousins had young families and knew the community and activities where Filipino families shared activities.

"My brother and I spent a couple of weeks looking at cultural centers that we had all discussed to see if Mom may want to visit. The family talked with Mom to assure her that she'd always be the most important part of the family. She need not fear going to a senior retirement facility. I said, 'Mom, we care about you, and although we work during the day, we will all try to get together for dinner more often. When you feel up to it, we'll take you to church. It's difficult for all the cousins to be with us, but sometimes they'll be here too.' She was quiet at first, then my brother told her that he would like us to visit his home too when she felt strong enough to travel in the evening. Then something we didn't expect, she began to cry. Mom hadn't cried much since my father died. But now she was older and in a different country without her surroundings where she had grown up. I hugged her and told her that we'd all be fine. She said, 'I don't want to be a problem. I only want my family.' I hugged her and almost cried. I wanted to reassure her, Mom, you're our family, and we're taking care of you. You don't need to worry. We're all happy you're here. You're not going anywhere.' Finding assistance for her during the day took a while because Mom spoke a bit of

English, but she missed someone her age who spoke Tagalog."

Many young people Lulu's age are juggling a new career as they complete their education. Listening to Lulu's story, I couldn't help but recall myself at her age and the responsibilities I'd assumed as a graduate student and new teacher. While my parents often needed attention, I had siblings to pitch in and help them. In more rural and multicultural communities, however, families live in larger intergenerational settings where family members can alternate care. When a senior is physically able, she or he helps to care for the grandchildren. In turn, the grandchildren assist in the care of older family members when they become ill and disabled. For me, Lulu's steady energy drove home the power of family and cultural connectedness. She acted on her commitment to accomplish what needed done to ensure the best for all.

Her family helped her to understand how she fit into their lives and that they shared her values of family and caring for each other. They were willing to reorganize their lives to create a more comfortable living place for Gloria in her infirm condition. Once assured that she fit, Gloria realized that they shared the values that mattered.

Maintaining family unity is involved and complicated for many immigrant families regardless of their socioeconomic standing. For seniors immigrating in their later years, family often represents the only security they recognize. Gloria's fear of being separated from her children and grandchildren presented major distress for her. Her children had immigrated at a young age. Lulu and her brother came as students and established connections with young people. Their lifestyles in the US posed a threat for Gloria. Revealing her fears to the family, though, showed her inner strength to advocate for herself.

Gloria's situation does not generalize widely. However, the insights of her story teach us about the resources that communities need for seniors who speak languages other than English. Additionally, the caretakers for those seniors also need support in dealing with family member in need of transportation and other services in their language. Lulu and her brother responded caringly to address Gloria's situation because they understood their responsibility as a family.

Since my early years, at different times I've been on both sides of the caregiving—needing a caregiver and giving care. As a child, I counted on my parents to carry out the role, as an adult I became one of their caregivers along with my sisters. On another occasion, when one of my sisters got cancer and my husband sustained critical injuries in a work-related accident, I became a caregiver. More typically, when friends are down with the flu or other illnesses, I take pots of soup, meals for the children, and give rides to the doctor. Being the primary caregiver in charge wasn't something that I'd considered having to do until I found myself in the middle of a friend's health crisis.

Sara called on a cold, overcast Memorial Day. No meetings for me to rush to on my calendar. "You're probably running to a meeting," Sara whispered.

"No, I have the day off today."

"It's me, Sara."

"I can barely hear you. You don't sound well at all."

"I'm having a setback. Can you come feed my cats?"

"Sure, but have you called the doctor?"

"I'll call tomorrow. I just need you to feed the cats."

I immediately drove to her house. I opened the back door with the key from the safe hiding place. As I walked into the dark, dusty, cold house, the stench of cat urine, smelly cat food, and musty mold assaulted me. In great dismay, I made my way past the kitchen and crawled over stacks of different size boxes stacked along the dark hallway. I sidled sideways to get to the back.

"Sara, where are you," I called.

"Here," came her faint voice. I turned on the light to her bedroom. She was lying in a bed tucked behind a tower of boxes and clutter. I had to step over rugs and clothes stained with blood.

Sara lived several minutes from my house. She had been one of the hummingbirds hovering over me during my serious illness twenty-five years earlier. She had meditated with me, taken me out to dinner, and driven me to doctors when I needed the help.

With tremendous shock, I shouted at her, "What is going on here? Where did this blood come from?"

"I've been vomiting."

"This is horrible. I'm calling 911."

She didn't refuse. In a soft voice she whispered to me,

"Tell them that I have diabetes and possibly stomach cancer."

As they lay her on the gurney, I sensed Sara release her preoccupations about her at home but not for her cats. Her last request to me was to feed Pepa and Deka. They rushed her to the hospital. I stayed behind to feed her cats and lock the doors. I was numb, processing what she had just disclosed to me. I drove myself home, wishing that I had only walked into a passing nightmare, but it was just the beginning.

When I arrived home, my husband listened to my story as I poured us both glasses of wine. "I'm afraid she's quite ill, and I don't know how to help her. She doesn't have family nearby. She has a niece in up north, who has her own problems. Sara says she trusts my experience with the medical system, but I'm going to need help. I'm calling her buddies Tony, Yoli, and Gina to see how they could help. I don't even know what kind of help she'll need when she returns home from the hospital. A brainstorm session is in order."

"I think you know what to do, but you need to take care of yourself too," Dudley said, "Be very careful with this. You just ended an exhausting contract with the Supervisor's office, and you haven't taken a break. Find out how much live-in care she can afford because you can't do the heavy lifting as she debilitates more. I'll help you when I can." His counsel about Sara sounded smart.

I visited Sara when she returned home from the hospital. She sat in bed feeling a bit stronger after a blood transfusion and some rest. She could again hold down a little soup and sip her Ensure nutrition drink.

From bed, her controlled voice blurted out, "They say I have liver cancer and congestive heart failure." The words rolled out from her mouth with resignation.

I reached down to hug her, "I'm so, so sorry!"

Without a word, sitting in bed, she stared ahead at the wall. We sat in somber silence until I stood up and told her that she needed to rest. "I'll be here tomorrow morning, and we'll put a plan in action to help you through this period. Treatments can be pretty tough."

"They don't know yet if I'll get chemo,"

"I'm sure you have many questions. I'll go with you to the oncologist."

68

"They told me to call for an appointment."

"Have you called Gina and Paul or anyone else?"

"I will tonight. Can I ask you something?"

"Of course."

"I don't have family or anyone close to help me right now. Do you think I could count on you to be my Power of Attorney for health? My doctor and the hospital want me to appoint someone. I know it's asking a lot of you because you work and you're not well, but I need someone."

"Yes, of course. We'll talk more about it. I wish I could stay with you tonight, but I can't. Do you want me to call someone"

She turned in my direction, "Not now. I'm OK. No one knows, and I don't want to tell anyone yet."

"You'll call me if you need me. I'm nearby." A slight nod of Sara's head assured me. "For now, you have these things at your side, fresh water in your sip cup, the phone, your novel, and TV control."

"Thank you. Can you feed the cats on your way out?"

"Sure."

Off came the dust mask and gloves as I walked down the driveway. Knowing that the mold and dust in the house stirred up my allergies, Sara understood my wearing them. She trusted that I'd be there for her, allergy mask and all.

For weeks, morning after early morning, I made my way to Sara's. Caring for her at home meant phone calls to her medical center to report her deteriorating condition and to schedule stomach treatments for her comfort. I raised my voice and demanded that she have an appointment with the oncologist as soon as possible. "She's very ill and needs to understand the full picture of her condition," I insisted. The nurse replied. "Dr. Omi doesn't have an opening before August 4th." My frustration peaked in a loud voice, "That's unacceptable! They've scheduled her for a myriad of treatments, and she hasn't even seen an oncologist who can give her an understanding of her condition. She must have an appointment soon!" But the appointment with the oncologist remained several weeks away.

Too tired to eat a late dinner in the evening, I gulped down a few tablespoons of mint chocolate ice cream and chamomile tea. Then I spent the evening reporting to everyone.

A couple of days later I heard Sara's whisper say, "I'm sorry that I'm keeping you from your office."

"Please don't worry. I'm organizing my schedule to be here with you." I leaned down and kissed her head.

That day I realized that Sara's resistance was weakening. After that, each day brought new problems to solve. Although she remained alert, more and more Sara declined physically. No longer able to drink even a sip of soup, she only requested to drink Ensure and water. Dudley and I drove her to the hospital for treatment to drain the fluid from her stomach, which had ballooned out. It took both of us nearly an hour to maneuver this mid-size, five-foot woman into his car.

After the appointment, at home, it took us one-and-a-half hours to get her from the car to bed. That afternoon I again broached the subject of moving to an assisted care facility. "You need round the clock care, and Gina and I can only be here during the day. Other folks can contribute an hour when their schedules permit, but it's only during the day."

Stoical about her situation, Sara suggested, "Maybe I can ask my friend Julia."

"She works during the day and has children to care for at nights."

"How about a home care agency?"

"They have to visit you here, and you'll have to meet the care home standards here in your home," Dudley explained.

Sara's diminishing attention span became apparent as we talked. She dropped the night care issue and said, "Hand me my mail, please."

Noticing her shorter attention span, I pressed her on the momentous decisions she had to make. "Sara, as your power of attorney for healthcare, your HMO requires us to answer some questions that you may feel are premature. It's best to talk about them while you're still strong enough to think about it. I need to ask whether you've given any thought to some of your final arrangements."

"I have a plot next to my family. I paid for a simple coffin." I felt an inner sigh of relief. One big item out of the way.

"I'm too tired. Can't talk anymore. Can we talk tomorrow?" She turned away from us and closed her eyes.

My husband left, and I stayed to wash her clothes and clean up around the kitchen sink and cat feeding area.

I wondered, with all the Buddhist and spiritual readings she had done, how she felt about this painful time of her life. By this time, I felt extremely sad that so much of our energy had been taken up by the day-to-day care for Sara. There hadn't been time for us to reflect on our friendship.

As Sara weakened, unable to sit up in bed without assistance, she developed one complication after another. Then, one early morning I received a text from Gina. "Been in Emergency Room with Sara since 5 AM. Hope they admit her."

I arrived at the hospital to find Sara in a private room. "How are you doing? What are they telling you?"

"Just more poking and prodding. The urologist is waiting for the blood tests."

"Rest. I'll find him." Outside of her room, I introduced myself to the authoritative-looking man walking toward Sara's room in a sterile white coat. He was the urologist. Together we walked into her room.

I held her hand while he described the test results. "Today's tests show that you have kidney failure. This is probably because your cancer has spread. Or it could be that there's a lot of pressure on the organs due to the liver cancer. Unfortunately, when this happens, there's nothing to do without creating more problems. I'm very sorry."

Sara listened with the same tolerance I had seen in the past months. I asked, "What does that mean, doctor? If you can't help her, she can't possibly go home. She doesn't have 'round the clock help at home,"

"I've scheduled the Palliative Care team to meet with you tomorrow." He locked eyes with Sara, who lay quietly in her bed. I held her hand. "They'll be in charge of your pain medications from this point forward."

Then she asked, "Does this mean I'm in hospice? Can I still drink water? I'm really thirsty."

Yes, of course. You can have anything you want. The Palliative Care team will explain it all to you," he replied. "We'll do everything possible to make you comfortable, so you won't have any pain."

"I want the last sacrament," Sara whispered.

"I'll arrange for a priest to come," I said.

Later that afternoon, a small group of friends stood quietly around her bed with as a priest performed the ritual. They held her hand and stroked her head.

Sara now slept long hours at a time. Three months since the ordeal began, doctors finally predicted her death aloud before she had an opportunity to consult with an oncologist, who could have given us the big picture at the beginning. In one of her brief awaking moments, she said, "I just want water and no pain." I squeezed her hand. She looked up at the ceiling, and two tears rolled down her cheeks. The end was near.

My dear friend Sara's remarkable grace throughout her illness gave me the strength to keep going as her caregiver during the most difficult and exasperating times.

After Sara's services, a few people privately told me that they had learned how important it was to plan before hand for health emergencies. They updated their wills and health directives. We all understand now that we can't expect to be able to care for ourselves when critical illness strikes. Some people spend years in chronically ill health, but others have little or no warning to prepare themselves. Sara had felt secure in her independence and the fact that she had friends to assist her. However, the unknown had brought an avalanche of decisions and bureaucracy for us to manage when the illness daunted her.

During an acute illness, the physical faculties, and rational decision-making abilities wane. A health crisis can easily overwhelm us no matter how prepared we think we are to deal with the demands.

Making decisions about where the best place is for someone to care for us becomes complicated if the senior adult needs to move to be with the caregiver, as did Lulu's mother. Moving from one's hometown to a caregiver's home involves significant physical and emotional adjustments for everyone involved. It can strain or forge relationships between the senior and caregiver as well as other family members. Most often, both occur. A stressful reorganization takes place as seniors and caregivers manage the new arrangement.

RB wore his wool hat and heavy coat, sitting in the front seat of the car he rode out of Belmond, Iowa. On that cloudy late January morning, the snow had stopped, but the air felt icy. It would be the last time he'd see his hometown, the only home he had known. His son Dudley drove him past his farm one last time.

Six hours later, RB arrived at a city he had only visited before, to a home that was not his and where he waited for three months. During this time, he accompanied Dudley to visit residential assisted living facilities until they decided on the right one.

When RB was forced to leave his hometown of ninety-six years to live in California where Dudley, who is my husband, could care for him, their relationship expanded. RB recognized Dudley as an adult and realized how much Dudley cared for him. My husband tells his side of how this geographic change for RB matured their connection. I became the assistant to the process and the observer in this new caregiver plan that involved our family.

For years Dudley had had traveled between Berkeley and Belmond to visit his father every few months. RB survived colon cancer, prostate cancer, a major stroke, and depression. Health complications persisted for him and for Margo, his second wife, who had chronic health problems. She used oxygen due to a debilitating respiratory illness, but her son cared for her health. Dudley, RB's only son, continued helping his father regularly to ensure that the two had the proper care at home. For specialist appointments, these two ninety-plus seniors drove themselves one hour to Mason City for medical appointments.

As he balanced his business and personal life, the years of flying back and forth took their toll on Dudley. He proposed various plans for his father within the limits of local resources for seniors with chronic medical problems. The couple chose to remain in their home, accepting minimal care from local meal services and a visiting nurse. Day by day they managed until the time came to make bigger life changes.

"Dad's care became my sole responsibility when Margo died," Dudley recalls. "He was left alone in their home in Belmond, where he was born, grew up, and became a very successful businessman until he sold his company and retired. He couldn't imagine living anywhere else. When Margo died, Concha and I returned to Iowa to be with Dad. By then, Dad needed a great deal of physical and emotional support. He was burying his second wife.

It was time for the difficult conversations. I knew that I had to convince him to leave his sizeable condo. Dad still served on the board of directors there, but now he had to move to California with us until we could find an assisted living facility. I had experience in senior care as a former administrator for a large senior retirement home in Oakland, and I felt confident that I could find him an assisted living residence near us.

I asked Concha to think about the possibility of this arrangement and what it would mean to our marriage and demanding workloads. I'm aware that such changes stress marriages. She felt strongly that Dad should come to California because, after all, he was family, and he couldn't care for himself. Dad realized that moving to California with us was the best solution and reluctantly agreed that he needed someone to care for him. Concha flew out to Belmond to help bring Dad back home with us.

In two days, RB filled two suitcases with all the things he felt he would need. Of all the personal decisions that he had to make, he was particularly concerned with his medications. RB deliberated over the kitchen tabletop of prescription medications. At the kitchen table, he sorted an array of cough medicine bottles. One by one he picked up each bottle and studied it, then set it aside. After examining several bottles, he took a breath and stepped aside, leaving all the bottles behind on the table with firm resolve. He mumbled, "Oh forget it, I just won't cough."

"Dad grew up during the Depression and worked the family's farm. Moving RB from his hometown meant leaving behind 96 years of his life history. He learned all about corn and at Iowa State, he developed hybrid corn seeds and became a successful businessman in Belmond. Although he traveled extensively around the country for business meetings, Iowa was home."

Dudley's experience as former director of senior care facility proved to be most beneficial as he began visiting facilities with his father. "Dad, you present well. That's what they expect to see. They want someone who has their wits about them and who will need minimum care."

After going from one facility to another, RB and Dudley chose an assisted living facility near Dudley's office. I took a different route on my commute in order to visit with RB a few times a week. Each time, I brought him the local newspaper and two cookies. On days when the quiet RB felt like talking, newspaper headlines filled the gaps. He especially treasured the local news from his friends at home and he appreciated hearing about Dudley's work. He wanted to be assured that he wasn't a problem for his son such that it would interfere with Dudley's work. He always seemed concerned about Dudley and wanted to see him succeed in his business. My father-in-law has a polite response to all of my efforts to engage him in talks about growing up during the Depression era on his farm in Belmond. "Some things are best left in the past."

Dudley visited his father during the week and took him to medical appointments. On Sundays, the three of us went on outings. We enjoyed lunch at our home with friends or a barbecue restaurant. Sometimes lunch at the dining hall in his assisted living facility filled the afternoon.

One evening Dudley came home and announced that RB had a girlfriend. We both looked at each other and had a good laugh. Dudley said, "I'm not sure, but I suspect that he may be personally interested in a woman there. I found this piece of paper, a phone number in the pocket of one of his shirts I was taking for laundering. Her name is Nellie."

"Maybe you should wait for real evidence. The lady might be one of his providers in the facility like a physical therapist."

A few days later Dudley gave RB the name and number he found. RB was relieved because he needed a haircut and had misplaced the name and phone number of a woman who came to the assisted living residence to cut hair. No need for further speculation.

Over the months that followed, RB adjusted. Having him nearby helped us feel like a family. He celebrated his 97th birthday in November at our home with a few friends. The family system was in place such that in the middle of December, Dudley and I went to Maui for a week's break.

Before our return, Dudley received a call from RB's assisted living residence. RB had a stroke and was in the hospital. After what had felt like an endless flight, we drove straight to the hospital. RB underwent countless evaluation tests. Dudley spent two days asking questions and wondering about the severity of the stroke. Finally, the news came, the stroke damage was extensive, and he would need a feeding tube.

RB chose to check himself into hospice voluntarily. Almost to the day, one year later, he made the same choice that his wife had elected to do when she had a stroke. We promised to stay with him around the clock. "Dad was in tears as he signed himself in and told the hospice nurse that he didn't want to be any problem for us because we were busy people with careers," Dudley said. "We assured him that we loved him, and we intended to be there with him."

RB asked to return to his apartment at the assisted living residence. My husband and I took turns keeping him company. "Dad was an intelligent and successful man, and he remained alert and inquisitive to the end," Dudley recalled. "As his strength waned, he talked less and less, but he asked one important question, 'How long does it take the body to die without water? I know the body can go a long time without food, but how long can it go without water?' That was a question none of us could answer. While he had a bit of strength, Dad called his 99-year-old sister, his best friend, and his cousin in Belmond to say his farewell. I wished he had told them how much he loved them, but he didn't. I'm sure they all knew."

I was emotionally exhausted from knowing the inevitable, and crying, so I stayed home to rest. The last night that RB was able to talk with his son, Dudley stayed with him all night. They talked of matters that RB felt he'd left unsettled. He talked to Dudley with confidence that he could handle what was left behind to be done, knowing that he didn't have to worry about his son. My husband said he felt very comfortable talking with his father all night. Neither one needed to sleep.

As RB's voice waned, he frequently looked at his clock and asked if it was Christmas yet. "No, Dad, today is December 23rd."

A day later RB's voice was even weaker. The hospice nurse visited every few hours to check on him and adjust his morphine. He continued asking if it was Christmas yet. We'd answer, "Not for another few hours."

Christmas day arrived. Dudley had to run to the office for a few hours, and RB asked to lie down. Since he'd begun on hospice care, he sat all day in his recliner with one eye on the clock and calendar. I sat in his living room with spiritual readings.

The night nurse walked by and ran to RB's bedside. "It's time! It's time," she called out to me.

"How do you know?" I asked.

"I've been present at this stage of life for many, many years,"

I called Dudley. "I'm around the corner," he said.

We held RB as he laid in bed. It was Christmas night, December 25th, and RB knew it. He was resting peacefully. His life was complete.

Moving his father across country made it easier for Dudley. Although RB felt isolated from his hometown, he was able to see his son in his family and work enough to recognize his life accomplishments. In turn, I got to know my father-in-law better. Life in Iowa was a frequent conversation, only second to his concern and love for his son. It was time to go home.

For many families, placing a loved one in a senior care facility can be an overwhelming ordeal. Decisions about affordability, location, and qualified residence staff, plus general environment can ambush caregivers and the parent involved.

Dudley's knowledge of senior residential facilities was a critical advantage for the family. He not only knew which assisted living residences to visit and the questions to ask the staff at the interviews with RB. Theirs was a fortunate situation, mainly because the San Francisco Bay Area has many senior residential facilities, offering families more choices from which to select given their circumstances.

Many parts of the country have limited possibilities and choices for seniors needing residential medical assistance. When seniors can't care for themselves and no one can care for them at home, as Gloria faced in the Philippines and RB faced in Iowa, these elders confront the need to move long distances from their home.

It's imperative for seniors to access the resources available to them for transportation and in remaining connected with others. Ultimately, staying networked with family and other seniors has positive results for older adults. In the absence of close family, seniors are forced to reach out to public assistance agencies when they're ill or suffering from hunger. Seniors residing in large urban areas are more advantaged because more social resources exist.

As convenient as it seems, older adults who have family members need to accommodate the family who will care for them. As happened in the story at the beginning of this chapter, relatives don't always embrace the idea of caring for a senior. Nevertheless, the grandson in the initial lore story represents the hope that the younger generation may demonstrate more compassion for seniors in our culture.

Almost everyone I interviewed lived with one or multiple medical problems such as heart problems, diabetes, stroke, cancer, multiple sclerosis, and complications. Some were chronic, others more acute. How these people dealt with health issues depended on many visible and invisible factors. Though fears and impatience exist while helping us to find our resilience, caring for our bodies is easier for those with access to adequate information and services. Regardless of the health care availability, the bond between people at a time of need provides the perfect setting to shape and reshape our deepest connections in our later years.

3

TRUSTING NEW REALITIES

Grandmother waited until the night was too dark for the soldiers to notice any movement because Hmong people would be shot. Grandmother led the families from our village to walk quickly across the mountain to the boats that waited for them. If we didn't leave on the boats in the dark, the soldiers would capture us. We ran part of the way and walked fast in other parts. When we reached the boats there were crowds of people waiting to board and leave before the soldiers caught up with them. People shoved and pushed, and Mom and Dad lost Grandmother. We didn't know if she got on the boat or not and everyone who could fit on the small boats got on quickly.

All through our journey, we couldn't call out to her because we had to be very quiet all the way. We arrived in Thailand early morning and they put us in buses and drove us to the camps far away from town. That's what we would call home for some years.

Every day was life of worrying and wondering if Grandmother was in the camps of hundreds of people.

Then one day a woman said that she had seen Grandmother in another camp. We searched for her until we found her. Grandmother had become ill, but she was so happy to see us. Finally, we were reunited.

Grandmother was brave enough to lead us across the mountain to the boats, and now she'll have to keep fighting to stay strong. She stayed in the camp with us, but she became too weak to make the trip to here to California.

Hmong families teach us how to invoke our inner strength. In relationship with others, we confront difficult situations, but it's possible to restore them. Opening new windows provides opportunities for us to empower ourselves. We're not always aware that life needs a new attitude or perspective. For that reason, I found the stories that Hmong people shared about opening new visions in their lives quite important.

Cai was a few years older than his younger brother, Kum, who was about ten years old. Since arriving at the coast of Central California, Kum began attending school and Cai made sure that he attended every day. At the end of the year, Kum received a perfect attendance certificate during a school assembly. At the end of the day, Kum ran home feeling overwhelmed by all of the attention he had received for his achievement and for having his mother, Mrs. Cha, attend the assembly dressed in full length, colorful, embroidered Hmong dress. The teacher had invited Kum's mother to the school assembly because it was a special day for him. Mrs. Cha sat on the floor in the back of the auditorium until a teacher offered her a chair. This was more attention than Kum could bear.

At home he sat quietly doing his homework at the kitchen table. Cai noticed Kum's behavior and talked with him. Cai knew what happened at school, and he understood how difficult it was for Kum to feel different and separate from other students who were not Hmong. Kum was born in the camps when the family was in Thailand before traveling to the US, so he had not experienced the terror that Cai and the family had. Cai felt it was his responsibility to tell Kum how fearful and horrifying life had been for them as they escaped from Laos.

Kum listened and heard from Cai while things could be tough for him in this school, the Hmong people had been brave through much bigger difficulties and lived through them.

It's possible to come to such lessons at different stages of our lives, stirred by people we never imagined helping us. Leaping into major life changes in our senior years takes a great deal of courage. However, some life events make changes imperative. Those directions engage us in fresh new ways.

While it was admirable for Frank and his family to practice a healthy lifestyle, I couldn't help realizing that a great deal of work remains to be done. Geographically, Frank and his family lived in a community where people's unhealthy lives are blamed on the residents. The dearth of adequate healthcare providers to those addresses makes this area a medical desert. Frank tapped into his early years to learn how to go from the private to communal responsibility.[1]

"Debra is under a fair amount of stress, and it's taken its toll on her. I've had to become her advocate and help her to manage her health care because the pressure has rendered her incapable of handling all the calls and visits to doctors and specialists where their offices were hours away. However, the medical situation here in the Rio Grande City is horrific. The doctors' offices are at least an hour's drive from here."

Frank's experience with healthcare began as a private issue until his family gave him a different perspective. Some people arrive at a new purpose in their lives rather unintentionally as did Frank. He surprised himself as he assumed responsibility for Debra that he'd never imagined.

"I found myself caring for Debra, my wife's, health issues at home more every day. Soon I was driving her to the doctor more frequently. This may sound funny, but until then I hadn't paid much attention to the fact that we had to depend on each other more and more because of senior age medical needs.

She went to see a doctor, and they told her to see a gynecologist for a complete exam. The gynecologist is a five-hour drive away to Austin because there's no one locally. She's had heart related complications with menopause, which caused more problems with balancing medications. It's been quite problematic for her now that she's in menopause because there are no physicians who specialize in those problems. Debra and I have always maintained that doctors around here in Rio Grande City just want to convince patients to accept the easiest solution to their medical problem so they can get Medicare to cover costs.

A few years ago, one of our daughters who lived with us had a stomach issue and the local doctor waited until it became an emergency before he took it seriously. When we arrived at the hospital with her, they told us that if the ulcer had been caught earlier, she wouldn't need to be there."

Frank's family, along with many residents in the area, faced the inadequacies of their medical services and realized that they had to take control of as much of their health as they could.

"We have to take care of ourselves the best way possible by reading and staying informed to enjoy a healthy life without doctor appointment after appointment. Debra and I have been pretty conscientious about food and diet. Plus reducing work-related stress in the workplace and trying to spend less hours working at home after teaching. Senior age has also brought some insults and challenges like my losing the ability to keep track of all the details like pin numbers. There are too many to remember. No longer is just one for a simple bank account. For me, the mental signs require noticeable changes. We eat right and reduce worrying because we don't have a lot of confidence in the doctors. Not having to drive hours to doctors' appointments saves lots of energy."

I resonated with Frank's good sense that we can take responsibility for our health care through good preventive practices. While health awareness requires becoming knowledgeable about helpful personal practices, the communal care of people rests on more than each individual family.

"I admit that there are times when I need a different perspective, and I call my mother," Frank said, "Living far from her since Dad died has made me reconsider how important it is for me to call and see her more often. Mom believes that I should care for my own family in every way. That's what makes her happy and me, of course. I feel a sense of harmony when I talk with her. She has a solid strength that she communicates in a calm way. I think it's her solid work ethic and faith that's kept her strong.

From the time she was young, Mom worked the fields picking almonds, blueberries, and apples, and all the crops in the area. For my sibling and me, the fruit fields around Wayne, Michigan were the family playgrounds while my mother picked crops.

She walked off the farm fields and took a more sedentary employment, working for Wayne County, Michigan. She worked for the county until she retired twenty years later. Finally, she had her well-deserved rest with a decent pension. She worked hard all of her life and I don't ever recall a complaint from her. It was all about ensuring that all of us, brother, and sisters, got an education and learned to be good people.[2]

On my recent visit to Michigan, I spent some time with Mom. She likes to get up in the morning and have her coffee and peacefully read the paper from page one to the end. She also belongs to a Pentecostal church, so she doesn't watch T.V. Her time is occupied with church activities. She lives for family events. She's played a very active role in helping raise her grandchildren, who have been very successful academically. It was most important to be present for her grandchildren, to be near them, and to watch them grow. She also helped my brother, who is a pastor, and his wife to build their church.

When my brother purchased a boy's club to rebuild as a church, I visited his church in this new location in the inner city of Detroit, down in the worst of the worst section. I was shocked when I looked out his office window. It's like a war zone. It could have been in a third world country. My mother lived with those values she taught us. Now she continued doing it by loving her family and serving community where my brother's church is located."

Frank's voice softened when he spoke of his mother. I sensed that he felt stirred by a sense of responsibility for others that his brother and his mother too assumed in their own ways.

"I returned home rejuvenated. I was ready to get out of my self and aging pains and helping the community to become informed about ways to remain healthy. Maybe I could also help community people organize ways to make good healthcare available here. Regardless of what the existing state or national healthcare laws provide, communities like this remain underserved. The older seniors in the area cannot travel long distances for the care they need. That has to change. Now I see that we've dealt with enough of this problem. We need to take action. I think some people around here are ready to help organize around this health issue."

More is written about food deserts than medical deserts. However, the concept merits the same urgent attention. Rural areas are more in danger of becoming medical deserts as medical cuts affect communities and towns in remote areas.[3] News editorials report that nearly thirty million people live farther than one hour from a hospital with an emergency care unit.[4]

Frank's personal experience made him aware of the unavailability of health services to rural communities outside urban and large metropolitan areas. Frank and his wife's time-consuming academic careers allowed little time for them to actively advocate for adequate healthcare in their community. However, they committed whatever time permitted to becoming informed about the local decision making for these services. Now as senior adults, they've become a part of a large percentage of their Rio Grande City, Texas neighbors in need of specialized medical services including cardiologists, gastroenterologists, orthopedics, urologists, and gynecologists.

Reconnecting with the values that framed his early years helped Frank to rethink his role as a senior in a community that needed his leadership to obtain specialized healthcare. On his visit home, his mother's nurturing pace of life near the soil where he resided reminded him of the backbone beliefs that had shaped his growing years of community work, collective support, and resilience.

Gracie's relationship with her family gave her a basis for how to shape her family practices in later life. She reminisced about the way her culture played a pivotal role in her day to today decisions.

Her grandmother lived with her family most of Gracie's life. The grandmother, the elder in the family, valued education, and she impressed upon Gracie the importance of schooling. When young Gracie moved with her family from Texas to the Bay Area, she felt very isolated in the neighborhood and in her school. Gracie and her sister attended an Irish Catholic school, and although all of the students were working class, Gracie and her sister were the only Mexicans. No other students looked like them or spoke Spanish to them. She recalls learning English quickly, smiling at all the students, talking to the popular kids, and studying a lot. Through a dismaying experience Gracie discovered a strategic way to belong, which later expanded the most important relationships in her life.

Gracie recalls that some changes in her early years taught her about living her in later life. She recalled, "I was a freshman in high school on that cold rainy day. I had to call home because I had forgot a book at home, and the only phone was in the principal's office. There I met up with many other students waiting for a pass because they were late. We all smelled of wet wool in our Catholic school uniforms. When it was my turn to use the phone, the office was still crowded with students. My grandmother answered the home phone, and I did not want to speak Spanish because I didn't want others to hear me. So, I spoke to my grandmother in English. She didn't say much to me. I went on with my school day until later in the evening.

I was doing my homework, and that call in English from the school pay phone in the principal's office haunted me. I had become ashamed of speaking Spanish, and I spoke to my grandmother in English. In our culture, that's 'falta de respeto' (lack of respect). She must have thought I was nuts. I had crossed the line. I crossed the line out of my shame. I rejected her, and I had rejected my culture.

The episode with my grandmother touched me deeply," Gracie confided. "Not because I felt guilty or disrespectful, but respect for elders was a core value for me as much as my grandmother. I just hadn't learned how to live comfortably between two worlds. That kind of understanding grew as I matured. When the time came, and I had my family, that incident became my inspiration for shaping my family. It's important enough that I instituted the family night dinner in my home. My sons and their families gather for a potluck dinner every Thursday night without fail. Most of us enjoy food, and we're good cooks. Everyone cooks something special. It's about sharing. Togetherness is a survival strategy for us. Having the strength of family means everything to me."

When I was a graduate student, I learned that when people acculturate to the point of neglecting their roots, they deny the core of who they are. That's the danger. Psychiatrist Arnaldo Solis[5] says that when someone denies their roots and they don't have the foundation that will help them be strong when they confront injustices in the place they live, they have rejected their foundation.

Anthropologist Angeles Arrien explains that in the later years, forgiveness is an essential quality. Through forgiving ourselves for participating in self-deception or abandoning ourselves to win acceptance and approval, senior years become more gratifying.[6] The incident in the high school principal's office made Gracie aware that she'd rejected her cultural values to feel accepted by her peer group. Gathering around food sets the table for communication that doesn't require words for Gracie's family. Family dinners continue the connections that meant warmth, respect, and support for Gracie throughout her life.

Early life values can shape later practices as culture evolves and grows.[7] In her senior years, Gracie's cultural ritual links the generations in her family together. Forming cultural continuity through meaningful rituals strengthens the overall life of senior experience.

The decisions and choices we make draw from many influences, and among the strongest are familial and cultural beliefs. Through their cultural back bones, Gracie, and Frank both found the strength they needed to move forward. Frank's relationship to his mother and Gracie to her grandmother built foundations of self-respect and care for themselves and others through family unity.

Angela shared a cultural connection with Debra and Frank when she felt physical symptoms related to menopause. That is, our culture helps us to interpret the situations in which we find ourselves. For many women, menopause signals early stages of what's casually called "old age." Angela knew that the change she was going through was a natural physical problem, yet she felt very exhausted by the symptoms. Why was this presenting such a problem now when this phase of her life should be long past, Angela wondered. She accepted her doctor's advice and medically treated her symptoms. While they abated a bit, Angela believed that this was just the beginning of what her senior years would bring. Angela learned that other cultures understood the same bodily condition very differently.

Mario Martinez, psycho-neuro-immunologist, has studied elders in many cultures around the world and observed that their beliefs about health related signs of aging dictated different responses.[8] In some cultures, these signs are embraced as a badge of honor. In fact, some cultures do not have names for some conditions that afflict us in this society. Regarding this aspect of menopause, he primarily portrays the Japanese culture and describes their diet and lifestyle as the main reason for low incidence of menopause related problems.

When menopause including hot flashes persisted, Angela felt frustrated as she'd used all the remedies recommended to her by experts or books. The hot flashes persisted. When her son visited home from medical school on a break, she gave him an earful of complaints about her situation. His response was not what she expected as she explained to me.

"Well into my 60's I began to feel menopausal and post-menopausal physical problems that I hadn't felt before. When my youngest son visited on his break, I couldn't stop talking about my health issue that was disrupting my life. After listening to me long enough, Phil, told me, 'It's all in your head, Mom.' I was expecting words of compassion and lots of understanding, not this response to what he thought was annoying grumbling. I had to laugh to hear him talk to me in that way that sort of pierced me. My gut went into somersaults so I knew there was something I should try to understand. If he was right what does it mean that it's in my head?

Does that mean that I wasn't getting old? How does one change her mind? That's crazy. Aging couldn't stop because I change my mind. It sounded simplistic, but important enough to talk to my son.

Phil laughed and gave me a big hug and said that he didn't intend to upset me but that there were other ways to deal with what I thought was an aging problem. He reminded me that people's bodies are bound to break down in some ways as we age regardless of how we feel about aging. However, the symptoms we feel in menopause don't have to be a problem. He showed me a section from one of his medical anthropology books. In that book there were stories of women from South America, Western Africa and Northern Europe. Their stories were about aging and menopause. Bose was from a country in Western Africa. She moved to the U.S. and began working in the medical field and saw many women coming into the office with symptoms of what was menopause. She didn't understand why this was treated as a medical problem. She asked other colleagues and learned that in this country, many women have stressful professions and lifestyle. While many doctors recommend the natural approaches to address the symptoms, many women, do have terrible problems and they need to function in their daily lives, so they seek medical attention. Apparently, in some countries, the medical system does not appropriate sufficient money for women to receive the needed medical attention for menopause. The Western African medical doctor talked about the African women who have had many children. They welcome menopause because it's a relief to know that they are through with the child-bearing years.

My curiosity about how older women in this country dealt with menopause pointed me to the one person that I had never talked to about this matter-my mother. My conversation with my mother was very informative. Mom was now in her 90's but she remembered living in a remote rural area where medical care was quite a distance, so menopause came and went. She said that she had been taught by her mother to ignore such problems because it was a natural thing for a woman to experience as well as a good thing. I had to believe that it was because it was a form of permanent birth control.

I thought a lot about what Phil told me, but I had to tell him that I appreciate that women in other cultures experience menopause differently, I had to think about what was right for me. Yes, I probably feel anxious about getting older, but I didn't have to grin and bear the difficult symptoms because I need to listen to what's best for my overall quality of life. Yes, I appreciate that women in other countries experience menopause differently, but apparently many don't have access to medical attention.

I kept reading and studying and learned to appreciate how other cultures honor elders and respect people when they age. Maybe that's why some women don't mind going through menopause. They look forward to being honored. In other cultures, an older person is revered so much more. You go to elders for advice. In this country, older people may have more medical attention than other countries, but we're often considered worthless and mindless. You become senile and get ugly because you get wrinkles and you are no longer an asset to society. I guess that's why some of the way I feel about menopause making me old is because I don't feel old and my body is doing these things that mean that I am, so it's a bit of a struggle, but I do want to change my attitude but I think it's more about growing older.

I look around and I see my mother who handles her age with pride and good humor. I want to feel proud that I get to become old too. I've worked so hard in my career and now that I no longer have that, I want to feel useful. My mother doesn't have any issues with who she is or feeling useful. There's pride in there. I'm partly in denial of getting older, I want to model my life like my mother and appreciate myself at whatever age I am regardless of how my body feels.

After I got comfortable with my body, I accepted it. I wasn't in denial of what my body was experiencing. I kept thinking that I'm going to be like my mom. I'm getting to believe that how you perceive becoming old is how you're going to age."

Angela reminds us that family members of different generations can hold different cultural beliefs. In his academic pursuits, her son had learned to understand health differently, though. Maybe he hadn't considered the bigger picture about women's access to medical care in other cultures. Her mother had learned a similar way of thinking, informed by her life in remote towns where medical access was limited. Angela is a good example of how it's possible to accept a new cultural perspective and responses to one's body's distress.[9]

Where is home when your family ties stretch across a continent? What keeps relationships strong with great distances between us? Norma felt she didn't have to answer this question because she felt equally at home in two countries.

When retirement time came for Norma, her choice of where to call home became clear to her. Norma never had any conflict with the places where she resided. She had strong connection with the places where she landed because her connections with her friends, family and work colleagues remained strong. Growing up in a Jamaican and Panamanian family, Norma has always been part of a very tight family both in Panama and in the US. She remained closely connected to everyone as though they all lived in the same town. When Norma retired from her work, she made a difficult decision to leave her children and grandchildren in the US for the place that had held her heart since her childhood in Panama.

"I'm very close to my family in Panama. I've always communicated almost daily as one of many siblings with many nieces and nephews and now of course, their children, my grand nieces and nephews. Either they call me, or I call them, email, text, sometimes saw them on WhatsApp.

Although I was very happy to leave home and strike out on my own to attend college in New York, I knew I'd miss my family in Panama. However, experiencing a little independence was refreshing. I won that scholarship to Skidmore College in New York. I studied psychology. I really enjoyed my college years, new friends, and independence. It was my new life.

The Vietnam War had just ended when I graduated from college and the job I had as a psychologist in Philadelphia working as a liaison between families and their children's school. I may as well have been in the poor communities in Panama. I questioned why this was allowed to happen in this wealthy country.

My boyfriend was in medical school. Once married, we respected each other's career paths. When he established his private practice, I jumped right in to help organize the office as his administrative assistant. That consumed all of my time. Meanwhile, my professional work took a back seat for what I thought would only be a brief period.

As his office was growing, my attention was with my two young daughters. I loved them and I wanted more than anything to give them all of my attention. I couldn't ignore the resentment that I felt festering from within when I thought of how much I had given up for him to have a successful practice. In my family all of us worked hard to develop skills and talents to obtain work that was satisfying, and my parents always admired everyone's talents. There was no prejudice against women having careers. So how did I find myself in this situation with a man that didn't support my career.

Tensions grew at home. One evening we had invited guests for an early dinner, and I was peeling cucumbers. My husband was preparing something else, but he began instructing me on how to peel them his way. I argued that my way was just fine, and he continued needling me about my method. I got so frustrated that I threw the peeler at him. Fortunately, it missed him, but it was the beginning of a miserable evening, trying to be pleasant with my friends while still steaming inside.

They say it's not squeezing the toothpaste that's the cause of married couples fighting. That's very true. In this case, it's not the tube of toothpaste, it's about peeling the cucumber. But it's not really about the cucumber or peeler either. I felt that I had spent years supporting him in setting up his practice while my career was on hold. I wanted to continue working and developing my expertise and got no support doing that because now my two lovely little girls had much of my attention.

My need for fulfillment grew to where I was forced to take a position because I knew my marital status was going to change. I took an administrative position in a school district and cared for my girls and home. We all had a difficult time with the transition. It didn't end my headaches. I had different challenges returning to work, but the house was more peaceful.

I admit to loving my work and growing with the positions that I had, working with low-income communities that needed my expertise. Then came the time when being a school principal became more stressful than how I wanted to live my life. I took a position as a teacher for a short time, which I enjoyed very much until it was time to retire. Yes, I wanted to go the retirement route and spend time with my family, including my new grandchildren, and read to my heart's content while taking different classes, which I didn't have time to do while working.

After retiring, I reveled in doing all I hadn't been able to do before. I traveled to Panama and stayed for longer stretches to visit with family without the pressure of returning to work. In the back of my mind, I thought of ways that I would translate my skills from all my previous work to new directions in ways I could serve people.

It was during that period an incredible thing occurred. One Sunday afternoon I received a call from one of my sisters in Panama. A horrible accident had occurred. Apparently one of my older nephews was driving a car near the house of one of my sisters. His foot accidently slipped and hit the accelerator. The car went out of control. It went up the curb crashing into the house where my sisters and her husband were standing by the door with bags of groceries. He struck them, killing my sister, and critically injuring my brother-in-law.

I couldn't breathe for what seemed like eternity. For days, my family and I were on the phone as they called to talk. There were many questions and few answers. Nothing made sense. I listened to the facts as all my family members were giving them to me as they understood them, but it was still incomprehensible. I only offered what I could from a distance. My nieces and nephews who had legal and professional skills were handling much.

I flew down to Panama for the funeral and stayed a while. I felt helpless except for listening and letting family members take sides in the matter that was clearly an accident. But so much history between family members took precedence. After talking with as many family members as possible I tried to help people mend their differences, but family factions were strong. I couldn't add anything to the matter. I knew it would take a long time to settle insurances. People's feelings were raw. They weren't listening to the fact that it was an accident.

When I returned home, I was still dealing with the tragic accident because calls between my siblings and me continued. I tried to rest but I felt like a zombie for a while. About that time, my older daughter brought a stack of brochures on retiring in Panama. Honestly, before then, I had no plans to do such a thing. Just reading the brochures made my other daughter cry. She said it was inconceivable that I would leave my daughters and grandchildren here. She said that if that's what I chose, they'd learn to live with it. I grabbed her and held her tight. I almost didn't want to let go.

It wasn't an easy decision for me. However, after a long while and many family talks, I felt sure that's what I wanted to do. The Panama family crisis was not the influencing factor for my decision. It wasn't my place to convince them of what they weren't ready to face.

When I announced to my family in Panama that I was moving down there, they were happy. One sister did have reservations that she felt had to do with how difficult it was for seniors to adjust to new routines. She cautioned me about making such a major change in my life at my age because older people don't adjust well to changes. My sister is much older, and she has had some falls and other frightening experiences that frightened her when she was away from home.

I felt happy to have the freedom to make this change in my life. I know my kids will visit me and I'll come up to visit them too. We'll Skype as often as needed, which is the reverse of what I always did with my family in Panama. It'll be an adjustment. Every adjustment can also help us all to learn and grow."

Norma's story of belonging to families across two countries showed her strength to build strong and secure relationships in an effort to maintain cultural ties.[10] They re-established their relationships with each other and their tribe, enabling them to live their lives to their fullest. Like a kaleidoscope, perceptions can change, expanding relationships and bringing them into balance. We're not too old to learn new ways of thinking and doing. Other stories share how relationships and connections with friends, colleagues, family, and community change when we accepted that through meaningful social connection, we can break limiting thinking that no longer serve us.

Dan and his wife Julie discovered their senior adulthood differently. They lived a short distance from Atlanta for many years. Their life together had been active with their respective work, church friendships, and volunteering in community organizations.

At the time of our interview, Dan, widowed, had already sold their long-time home, and moved into an assisted care facility closer to Atlanta. Neither he nor Julie had children or relatives who could care for them. Their active years of successful careers and Julie's debilitating health had quickly transformed their comfortable lifestyle.

"Since I moved in here to this assisted living home, I've been using a walker. The doctors tell me that it's possible for me to recover a lot of my strength with physical therapy. Knowing that I do that every day here with some very friendly therapists. They take good care of me in this skilled care home. I wish I had been able to bring my dear Julie here when she was ill, but we couldn't afford to have both of us living here.

She didn't want to stay in an assisted living facility without me. She was afraid to be lonely. I'm in the assisted care home now is because I don't have anyone to care for me at home anymore. When she became more ill with that awful disease, they said it wasn't MS, but it was a neurological type disease like it. When it happened, I still worked at the insurance office that I had done most of my life. I had received an award for selling the most of any sales person. I worked very hard in my job, and it meant a great deal to me. Julie knew that my work was necessary to me. I didn't want to give it up. The social worker helped me to find helpers to help me at home, but from the beginning, I was exhausted doing all the care. I hired a woman to stay with Julie at night, so I could sleep a few hours and get up to do it all over again. But it wasn't enough. The sisters we have in other states have their own health problems.

Julie had always been very supportive of me doing my work, and I had supported her in her work too. Without children, caring for each other had become the most important thing for both of us. We had always been happy working and taking care of each other while enjoying friends and volunteering. After Julie retired from her preschool teaching position, she spent many hours volunteering at the Cancer Society Thrift Shop. She sorted clothes and priced the donations. Little by little, I saw her weaken and become unable to keep up with the daily chores around the house, so I began taking more time off from work to take care of her and help around the house. Without pay for my time off and the mounting bills for Julie's treatments, I admit that sometimes I felt depressed, and other times I felt angry that our lives were being disrupted in this way. My anger turned to guilt then I felt guilty that I was upset at the situation. I felt very badly for Julie and didn't fault her, but I wasn't ready to give up my life as it was.

One day we were driving home from her doctor's appointment, Julie said that she should apologize for making me give up so much. I felt so low that I could barely keep my hands on the steering wheel. I didn't know what to say because I realized that she knew how I was feeling, although I had never said anything to her. Then I heard myself say, 'I'm very sorry too. I'm sorry that you're in so much pain and distress. I'm sorry that the illness has robbed you of the life you loved. I'm sorry that the future you looked forward to enjoying is now filled with pain, but I'll help you all I can.'

'Yes, I know dear. And I'm sorry for us both, and I'm worried for us too.' The rest of that trip is a blur because all I could think was how I had been making my feelings more important than my wife."

By revealing her guilt feelings to Dan, Julie had opened the door for him to share his hurt as well. Revealing his distress about her illness set an honest tone for their relationship, which proved critical in their life together as they went on to deal with both of their health problems.

"Things became very difficult for Julie and me because of my problems with arthritis. I still got around, but the pain was unbearable at times. The doctor gave me meds. I could take care of both of us most of the time, but we had to hire another woman to help her. I called a homecare agency a few miles from the home, and they came out to assess the needs and see if they could help us. So, because of both of our needs, we now had two women who were assisting us. It helped because Julie's needs seemed to increase by the day. With two women helping us, that took most of the small savings we had. I stopped paying attention to how much it was all costing as long as I could pay each one when they were due to get paid. I watched Julie's health deteriorate quickly, and I'm glad that I did spend more time with her. Sometimes all I could do was hold her hand or get her water to sip. In the end, things got quieter, and she just wanted me next to her."

I felt touched by how Dan and Julie's intimacy grew. His compassion had blossomed day by day, giving way to the deep grief that ensued. These difficulties sometimes associated with caring for a spouse at home may prevent a spouse from caring for the other. Nevertheless, able spouses do accept caregiving responsibilities as Dan assumed.[11]

"When she passed, I was very, very sad. I spent days inside without going out for anything. If all I had was a can of soup at home, that was enough. Food did not interest me. One of the ladies who helped Julie came to visit, but I knew she was checking on me. She noticed that I wasn't doing well. When she saw the condition of the house, she offered to help me. She talked to me about some options for senior care facilities where I could get medical attention and not worry about keeping up a house. It sounded like a gift from heaven.[12]

I sold our house because I couldn't care for myself very well. The social worker helped me to get into this senior place. I had to move away from my small community to Fulton County. There was an appropriate assisted living home that accepted me. That's here where I am now. I was sad to leave some of the people I knew, but they didn't come around much after Julie passed. I was glad not to have to live in all the memories of Julie and the life we had.

Here they prepare good meals for us. I don't worry about keeping healthy food in the house. They take good care of me here, and with lots of people around me, I don't feel as lonely. We have meals in the dining room. It's a pleasant place to talk with others."

When people are young, making friends is effortless. We ask the neighbor kids to play ball with us or go to a movie. We eat lunch with someone by just asking him or her to sit with us. Things change as we age. We may need to put more effort into social inclusion, and family and friend networks shrink as some leave the area. Seniors with family members to assist them find some level of security. Without children or close family members to support us in the later years we may need to rely on professionals. Experts on homecare can help us take the next step, as Dan did, because on some level, we know that connection contributes to personal wellbeing.

Senior living facilities count on the fact that belonging is a vital part of well-being, especially as we age.

Dan and Julie coped with the physical and emotional stress due to diminished mobility and financial reduction. Through this period, they rediscovered togetherness in their spousal relationship, which resulted in major changes to manage their health.

At the assisted care facility, Dan found companions and friends that engaged him in things other than his health. His loneliness made room for friendship. He welcomed the wisdom of his choice to rearrange his life by living in a community with others whom he came to embrace as friends.

The family dynamics happened quite differently for Kyla. "I'm a baby boomer hitting sixty getting life in the right direction, and I know now that I don't have to be in a cluttered mess," she said.

As Kyla had entered her senior years, her health was strong, and her teenage children were relatively young. Yet a few years after her divorce, her family relationships posed many unexpected emotional challenges for her. She spoke of the struggles that redefined her relationships with her children. She hadn't expected that she would be dealing with healing the distance between them and herself resulting from her divorce.[13]

Referring to her divorce, Kyla said, "During the summers, my ex and I take turns having the children stay with us. During the school year, they are in Bloomington, about an hour away. My two daughters are in college nearby, and my son will complete high school this year. I visit them on Monday and Thursday nights, and on weekends they come up here. It was an arrangement that was a great sacrifice for me. To this day, it still surprises me. I never imagined not being with them every day each day. It had just never occurred to me at all.

A couple of years after the divorce, I went to my ex and I said I was dating and trying to get the kids to have a relationship with my new friend. More problems ensued. He became very bitter about it. He let the kids believe that somehow, I had left them all, the entire family. It kept playing out that way, even with our friends. I was frantic for several years. We had been divorced for seven years, but I became desperate trying to talk to my kids and talk to him.

To find some equilibrium with my relationships, I went to a therapist. I began figuring out some things by writing letters to myself. After writing the letters, I saw how the frustration and exasperation were leading me to a nervous breakdown. She was outstanding support. Something had to change. It was helpful, and during the final part I asked my ex if he could come with me. He agreed and we met for what the counselor called the mediation session. We decided that we would have to move ahead because I expressed feelings of being very frustrated and there were some things that he felt the same about me. We needed to overcome this. We couldn't continue this way. He admitted that he was feeling anger at the very beginning. I shared how heartbroken it had all been for me."

Kyla's voice sounded more intense than the circumstances suggests. When she spoke of the emotional outburst with her ex-husband, she choked up a bit. She realized that the divorce had solved only one of her problems. For years, she had been dealing with the emotional impact that the separation had on her children as well as her ill mother and disabled sister who counted on her.

"Of course, I have strong feelings about everything that has come down, but we tried very hard to be civil around the kids. When I was home alone, I broke down that's why I pushed for us to do counseling together."

I listened to Kyla explain that their amicable demeanor was due to the fact that they were both professionals. She continued, "I realized that dating had to stop. My relationship had to end. I couldn't have my relationship with my children and my partner together because they weren't getting along. I realized that I couldn't have it all. I can't have relationships without my kids being involved.

I feel like I'm growing into my own and I've also had to postpone some of my writing which has always meant so much to me, and I've put it on hold. I'm getting better organized and feeling at peace and creativity returning. I have some ideas, and I think it's time to get back into the writing. It's time to get to the ideas and all the articles that didn't get written. Those things have just been put on hold for too long. There have been too many things in my life all at once. Too many responsibilities have cluttered my days and months. It's time to grow up.

It's time to mature and say maybe I'm putting on too much. I'm making a muddled mess, and I no longer feel that I need to get rescued or that I am poor little me as a victim. I removed those blinders or psychological barriers that have been strewn in my path for so long.

It's time to put things into place and to be able to feel confident in my administration work for as long as I decide to keep working. In the world and particularly in this society where we live, it's a cultural thing to put on your calendar more than you can physically do, but act like you should be able to do them. I have to accept that I have to see that the work is too much, and it's not my perception it is too much. There's no way that I should be able to do everything. I am not going to stay up nights. It's unrealistic if I have to drink coffee and to take some a substance to stay awake. I won't. I don't do that. It's not healthy. It's not what I want to model for my children either. They see me being very busy, but when I am with them, I am with them. I don't spend a lot of time saying, 'I'm sorry,' or 'leave me alone.' I make very deliberate efforts to appreciate being with them. That's what gives me joy.

I want to be able to have the insight, the wisdom, and understanding to know that I've gotten wiser. I think it's important be able to do things and not judge yourself if you make mistakes. I don't beat myself over my situation with the kids. They need more of my time and I want to be there for them when they need me.

As part of the older generation, I feel we need to inspire the younger generation. I encourage my students in the classes I teach to speak out against any injustices. They can at least find something to get involved with like activities that expose them to issues of xenophobia and racism or whatever else is happening around us. I think this generation will take a long time and a lot of education. I'm glad to be with them until I decide to leave this position. We need to connect young people with families to establish more personal relationships with those in different communities.

I'm not a sage by any stretch of the imagination, but I have reflected, and I think the idea of being aware is the wise thing. And I do believe that there's a lot to offer which is why I also chose the job that I am in. I didn't want to keep complaining. Then I thought I've been around the block a few times, I've worked at different universities, I have seen the things that make people thrive in their work and I think I can do that and that's because of experience. Yes, you can thrive at any age. Old means you now have this body of experience to tap."

Kyla's meaning of old, that we can thrive because we have a body of experience brings to mind Einstein's sage words, "We cannot solve problems with the same thinking we used to create them." The statement presupposes that our conscious mind is aware of the difficulties in which we find ourselves. To navigate the way to a solution requires us to access life's experience, just as the Hmong grandmother braved the terror surrounding her in order to lead her family to safety and a new life.

We find that strength in Angela, Norma, Dan, and Julie's stories, as well as in Kyla's. They transform their experiences as victims to compose new realities. The ability to trust the new reality we create, both derives from and enriches our knowledge.

PART II

IN SERVICE OF OTHERS

4

FOR THE QUALITY OF LIFE

The clouds covered the Oaxacan sky in Mexico. When the sun completely disappeared the from small town where Miguel lived with his family, he and his friends kept playing near the school. Then they began chasing each other, and they ended up near a cave. They continued chasing each other around until they tired. Heading home in the dark streets, they got lost and began to feel afraid.

The Curandera (town healer) Cuca, saw the boys walking down the street. They looked scared, and she convinced them that she could help them. She asked them where they lived. Then she took them to her home and helped them to find their way home in the dark.

Curandera Cuca walked each of the boys to his home. The parents were frightened for the boys. When Miguel knocked on the door, his parents grabbed and hugged him. His older brothers ran to scold him about staying out late. "We've told you many times to get home early. We called and called for you. Where were you?"

Miguel explained, and when he was through talking they noticed that Curandera Cuca stood behind him.

Parents knew the Curandera because she was the older woman who had helped the town to get streets so that the older people didn't hurt themselves. She had healed many broken bones because the cobble stone streets were difficult for many older people. This night she had helped the boys to safety. Curandera Cuca had two important roles, to heal people's health problems as well as the community's matters.

Who are the curanderas in our time? They're the workers whose mission it is to serve their community. In the context of aging, they're the senior adults who organize voter registration for elections. They're top directors at senior centers, seniors helping to house advisory boards and the directing community health centers, and senior parents educating younger parents about their children. Sometimes under financially distressed conditions, and in some cases despite poor personal health, many adults in their later years persevere to remain healers and leaders for change.

In spite of some senior adult's desire to continue serving their community, they confront negative ageism toward older adults in community leadership positions. Encountering such discrimination discourages some of them from continuing their participation in their community. discriminatory practices call for intergenerational education at a community level.

Senior adults with strong social ties and a history of service in community activities contributed to positive relationships and successful ageing.[1] Longevity, in turn, benefits communities where volunteer engagement declines in the younger age groups. It's well known that connections with community dwindle in the later years. Those who have been active in their communities would love to remain active, but declining health often interferes with their activism.

At eighty years of age, Corie often overlooked her chronic health problems to coordinate the community center and serve the families. She describes her community, "Many people are in such dire poverty here in North Richmond that seniors have made the news when they become ill from consuming dog food to reduce food costs. That was written up in the papers," she says. In this California community where most of the residents live on low resources and without access to healthy food markets nearby, the area has become a food desert.

Corie's leadership in North Richmond remained constant in spite of the autoimmune health conditions that plagued her asthma, diabetes, and lupus. These health problems commonly exist in underserved populations like North Richmond, which is plagued by a high incidence of poverty and surrounded by oil refineries and other polluting industries. Often in such underserved communities the health care systems are deficient. When major hospitals close residents are forced to travel longer distances in emergencies. These factors contribute to chronic health problems and absenteeism in the workplace. The absence of accessible medical care in such a community renders it a medical desert.

Since she was a young girl in Arkansas, Corie's life has revolved around working to assist her family, church, neighbors, and community members. Those values run deep in a family's tradition of practice in the church. From her early years, Corie's family made their home in North Richmond, where her leadership in the church led to her outreach to underserved families. She married and raised her family in North Richmond while maintaining a strong commitment to improving life for other families.

"This is the community where I live, and I love it. I want to serve it the best way possible as I have done since I was a young girl living here with my mother and grandfather. My church always reminded us to serve those in need. I worked with youth in the Neighborhood Youth Corp and other jobs helping families in need. My children and grandchildren have learned the same values about taking responsibility for our brothers and sisters. They all know how to stand up for people's rights.

Before I became Director of the Neighborhood House, I had worked there as staff. Since 1960, it's served the broader area. Founded by the American Friends Services Committee, a Quaker group, initially, it represented the African American people and low-income families. Afterwards, our agency became a refuge for Southeast Asians and Mexican immigrants during the urban migration of 1975. The Neighborhood House became a multicultural place for families of all racial and cultural groups that live in our greater Richmond area.

Our Senior Center, that was part of the Neighborhood House that closed, and it's where I'm Director now, has always been located in North Richmond.

When I became Director of the Neighborhood House, I made it clear that the Center would serve everyone who lived in the North Richmond and Iron Triangle areas in Richmond. For a long time, mostly African American folks lived here, but now we're more diverse as many Latino and Southeast Asian families have moved here. We welcome and serve everyone who comes through those doors."

Becoming director of the Neighborhood Community Center, Corie could help create a department for seniors that, given the severe financial cuts, survives as the only viable program. Seniors appreciate the services that the Neighborhood House provides so much that for one Christmas-gift-and-food give away a senior felt so special that she reportedly went to a thrift shop to purchase a skirt before she picked up her gift.

For many years, young people received services after school, including literacy classes, computer training, outings, field trips, and counseling. There they met other young people interested in doing good deeds. Adults received health services, classes, hot meals, and food baskets. Seniors were offered craft classes and stayed for a hot lunch, delivered daily by the canteen organization to the Neighborhood House daily. "Young people also worked with seniors," Corie told me. "They mentored each other. When the economy tanked, we lost some programs for seniors and the jobs of those people who ran those programs. Against our hopes that the money would return, the county and other funding continued shrinking.

Most of the essential programs at the Neighborhood House except for the Senior Center were cut. Fortunately, they kept the Senior Center open and made me Director. We've just continued operating as the Senior and Family Neighborhood House of North Richmond. Seniors and families can eat a hot lunch and take home a bag of food, and volunteers also help them apply for Cal Fresh if they haven't signed up for food stamps.

People have pride in this little community. It's had a reputation for being run-down. Our County Supervisor supports our Center in every way possible to change that image. We received funds to paint the inside and repair our roof and make other repairs around our building. We're truly grateful. Volunteers donate their time and resources to help clean up the outside and grow a garden. A neighborhood organization helps to maintain it and the fresh vegetables go to the seniors and families who need them.

At Christmas, I pull together gifts from many agencies, including the fire department, generous churches, and the other county service organizations. We open our doors here for over 700 families to sign up and receive Christmas food baskets, books for our local school children, and even gift cards for the North Richmond families.

The Lord has kept me around for many years. I'll be eighty-years-old soon, and my health weakens, sometimes. I have to slow down, but I'll keep pushing along as long as the good Lord permits me."

Meeting with Corie began and ended with a warm hug as though we were family. Hearing her talk about her health problems while continuing to organize her community, I admired her tenacity and commitment to her community. I couldn't judge her for working despite her serious health problems. I recalled that I was much younger when I overworked through a period of poor health and pushed my body beyond its limits. I spent years on crutches and in a power wheelchair while working as a university professor. Still, I continued to teach and research full time because I believed my work had social justice impact in communities. Corie's work has also been energized by her love to change the conditions of her community so much so that she sometimes overlooks the stress on her health.

This speaks to the cultural change needed to help women balance work and personal life. Many women are expected to work doubly hard to prove themselves in the workplace. Additionally, some work areas expect women to provide emotional and physical comfort beyond their professional duties.

Corie described, "The poverty is tremendous here, but our little Senior and Family Neighborhood House does everything possible to do to keep the doors opened. We knock door to door and appeal to the County organizations for funds. Yes, we do work hard, and I do have problems with my health, but I would feel worse if I stopped doing it.

A few other people and I have volunteered much of time to ensure that people in this community know that we're here to serve and we care about them. It's important to ensure that people don't lose hope."

While Corie's community work puts her face to face daily with those whom she serves, there are other ways in which older adults participate in social action and contribute to social change.

Anthony has spent a lifetime teaching, counseling, contributing to building schools and schools and finding new directions for underserved students.

"I'm so grateful that at eighty-eight, I continue counseling and teaching meditation to undergraduate students. I expect I'll remain working until I can no longer get to the classroom."

Anthony's inspiration to serve youth by teaching and mentoring evolved from the values that shaped him during his early years. He reminisced about the years of emotional trauma that opened doors to lessons he wouldn't have learned otherwise.

"I still remember my mother's words, 'Your dad says I'm no longer his wife, that he found somebody else.' She was looking at me, hugging me, trying to comfort herself and me. She couldn't hide the pain in her eyes, her sadness. She said that he put three dollars in her hands-one for my two siblings and me. A day or two later all of a sudden, she starts screaming and I guess she had a breakdown. She went to bed. She sat alone with three kids in depression. It must have been overwhelming for her. She was in bed for about three days. Then she got up and worked for us. From there on, she devoted her life to make sure that we had a good and safe home.

Shortly after that she developed a severe strain of tuberculosis and had to go to a sanatorium. My sisters stayed with my mother, and my brothers went to my great-grandmother, and I went to my godmother. After getting past the shock and the loneliness, I tried settling into life with my godparents. They were a well-educated couple that didn't have children, so this kindergarten kid was like a playground for them, but I missed my mother. They stressed schooling and studying and tried to make things fun. In spite of the fact that they always had good food in the house, and they kept me safe, all I wanted was my mother.

I fought against my godmother's wishes to adopt me. It played out in my school behavior where putting girls' pigtails in inkwells was fun, but it meant problems for my godparents. Somehow, I got through elementary school years with the help of my buddies. My godparents made plans for me to attend a strict Catholic high school that accepted me. It turned out to be a pretty good place for me. They helped me succeed academically, and I liked it. Pretty soon I was receiving accolades like admission into the California Scholarship Federation.

About that time, I began hearing questions like, 'What do you want to do?' 'What do you want to be?' I had heard someone say that his plan was to be an engineer. Although I didn't know what an engineer did, it was a way to stop them from asking me. More importantly, my godfather became proud of me.

A short time later, it was clear that engineering and I were incompatible. I liked liberal arts. All the subjects like English, literature, and language spoke to me. I also liked religion. I had religious brothers at my high school who were terrific teachers. They were my inspiration. I knew that I wanted to be a teacher as a religious brother. I knew that it meant me giving up getting married and having a family. I prayed to God for help in this decision, one I could not make myself even with those closest to me that watched as I tried to navigate my college years.

My godparents wanted me to consider the priesthood, but that didn't interest me. I preferred the teaching part of the brotherhood. Initially, Mom supported my decision, but when it came time for me to go away to college in northern California, my history of rejection in the earlier days surfaced. Dad leaving us and Mom sending me to my godparents left an imprint in me.

I did pretty well in college, but I got too big for my britches. In the brotherhood, I thought that teaching was going to be easy, but it required so many more skills. I worked hard to change it. I went to St. Mary's College. I related to the mission, the history of the institute, its ideals, its culture, and what it aimed to do, which was to educate youth.

After college, I taught high school, where most of the students came from poor families. They taught me about responsibility and caring for the poor. I saw the school's decision to accept mostly middle-class students and dismiss students from low-income families. I protested as much as I could, but they didn't change their policy. So that became the call for me to help open schools for the poor. That was the right thing to do for social justice. At that point, I knew I had to teach in a school that treated students from poor families as equally important as other students.

I began my mission by taking a position at Southside High School and advocated for students who needed a break in life. It was the right thing to do. One year later, I returned to St. Mary's High School that I had left. The administration and I tried to work together more cooperatively. It was short-lived.

My miracle position found me. An administrator at St. Mary's College in northern California called me to teach meditation and Spanish. I enjoyed the students and the subjects that I taught. I felt I'd come home. That's been my professional home since 1975.

Shortly afterward, I began working with a school in Tucson, Arizona. This became an essential part of my life's mission. I still go to a Cristo Rey school, a school dedicated to teaching students from low-income families. I've adopted them as much as they have valued my work. The kids that come are from low-income families, and they're all on the same level, so they all know that, so there's no problem there. They work five days a month once every week-one week is twice-to pay for their tuition. The tuition is $7,000, so I think they earn about $5,000, and the parents put in the other and then there's also financial aid. Also, it's college prep, and most of the students end up in college. When I visit the school, I plan to assist them in using meditation systematically. What's good is that finally, the teachers know that it's a tool that works. One of the teachers now knows how well this tool works and he's beginning to use it daily. He's starting to realize the power for achieving.

Last time my colleagues and I visited the school and talked to the class, 'What's happening since you began meditating?' the students shared how they had improved. They said, 'We participate more in class. We also have more confidence and better insights, and we work better together.' Some of them were repetitive, but that's good because that's what they saw. You could say that the five minutes a day are working, it helps them to achieve all they have done. I'm very proud that those students have kept up this discipline and have changed their lives.

When a colleague talked to me about the Wright Institute, I was ready for a new opportunity. I wanted to understand how my early life problems with my family contributed to my career interests. I got accepted into the doctorate program, and I spent a few years intensely working on my dissertation.

There I met Jose Martin. He was a part of a Christian order who left to become a Buddhist. He was charismatic, with unique healing gifts. When I met him at the clinic one time, I remember that he put my hand on his heart to show off. Well, he put his hand on my heart, and he took my breath away. I said, 'What's that?' He said, 'That's Reiki.'

In 1991, I became a Reiki master after completing all four levels of training. I met a lot of people who were interested in learning from me. The people that most come to me are the workers at St. Mary's college, the Mexican workers. They just wanted to have a spiritual moment. And of course, the Bishops came out against Reiki, it's supposed to be a New Age thing, which is not true. It's based on Buddhist practice of hundreds of years ago as well as science.

I had seen many birthdays when I had to retire from teaching full-time in the Psychology Department because of stomach cancer. At my age of eighty-years-old, I'd come to a life and death opportunity to apply everything to my healing, which I had taught to others in my work. Thank God I made it through that tough period.

When I felt stronger, I continued teaching meditation part-time at the college. Most of my teaching, however, has now been focused in doing workshops. I had weekend workshops on campus and accepted invitations to travel to other countries to teach meditation to university faculty as well as students. I've gone to the Philippines twice so far, to four universities there to teach meditation. I also travel to Mexico City, Costa Rica, and other places to conduct invited workshops. And of course, I continue going to Tucson, Arizona as often as I can."

Twists and turns in family life caused by financial stressors and residential opportunities influence our perception of the world. Anthony's career choices led him to a mission that defined his work to the present. How later years unfold and how personal values shapes the type of work that keeps us passionately involved often begin in our early years.

At eighty-eight-years-old, Anthony travels nationally and internationally to conduct meditation classes wherever he is invited. "My life's mission is about serving by teaching young people. Social justice work is important to me. I don't accept the limitations of retirement according to the age limits. I'll work as much as it takes to do the work I see needed. Who cares how much time it takes? It's our love for others that produces the results that matter. I'm glad that good genes run in our family."

To care. To help. To partner. To lead. Seniors make a difference in as many different places as there are places that need leadership. They work in our communities, in counties, and sometimes in causes that impact the larger society. There's a great deal of work to do as activists, whether it's planting heirloom rose seeds, serving as an advocate on a state level Food Policy Council, or working with advocate groups to protect the land and water. Whether older adults remain in a career and the workforce or choose to leave it, and wherever they reside, they do make a difference.

Such was the work of the Ojibwe people on their Water Walk. Christina's connections with this group provided an opportunity to participate in their annual ceremony to honor clean water. A group of Ojibwe elders that lives near Lake Superior invited her to join them to talk about her community work and to learn more about the Ojibwe water walk. Cristina's work as a community psychologist, educator, and elder was known in the Ojibwe groups. The grandmothers taught self-respect, identity, and belonging to young adolescent women reaching womanhood in this complex mainstream culture.

Christina had a few opportunities to appreciate the Ojibwe people on her visits with them. "In Ojibwe culture, the women are the keepers of the water. The problem that the Ojibwe intend to continue healing involves the many cases of abuse of the water in Michigan around the Great Lakes. The people believed that their grandmothers unified the tribes." The elders believed their intention and action unified the people and tribes.

The Great Lakes are the largest group of freshwater lakes on the planet, but their future is uncertain. Every year, Christina told me, Native Americans called the Mother Earth Water Walkers trek hundreds of miles around the Great Lakes to raise awareness of water issues in the region.

"I was honored to be invited by the Ojibwe band. I was invited to be with them as many did the Water Walk in Michigan's Lake Superior. I visited there four times. We were on Medellin Island in the Great Lake there three or four days. Unable to walk with them I witnessed the Walkers brake up into many small groups. The Water Walker grandmother was among them. She was the elder leader who first began walking because she felt it was an important ritual to save the lake's water. The role of elders in their community is of great importance to me. It's noble that they teach their young members to live a clean life and care for the water, which they did in their annual water walk ceremonies. The Ojibwe tribe intend for the annual traditional Water Walk to call attention to the critical need for clean water."

The Water Walk is more than a call to action. It's a spiritual journey that connects all who walk it to each other and to the respective indigenous tribes. Walkers chant, and in some walks, they celebrate the gathering with their traditional Native Healing ritual, also known as the four directions of the wind:[2]

Mother earth, hear your child,

Be a bond between the worlds of earth and Spirit.

Let the winds echo the knowledge of the grandmothers,

Who await, unseen, yet visible if I only turn my eyes to the world.

Let me hear their voices, in the winds that blow to the east.

From the East: I seek from the place of the rising sun

To see with the trusting innocence of childhood,

The lessons of Spirit,

Given in love of our Creator.

From the South: to learn the ways of questioning.

The fire of independence of adolescence,

The truths, and how they help us

Grow along this path.

From the West: where the grandmothers teach us

Acceptance of responsibility

That come during the years of marriage and family.

That my own children grow strong and true.

From the North: where elders, who by their long lives

Have learned and stored wisdom and knowledge

And learned to

Walk in balance and harmony with our mother, the earth.

When I attend cultural celebrations where the spiritual ritual of the four directions of the wind unites those gathered, I'm moved by the connection that the ritual evokes in us. We connect to one another in the present life and to our loved ones who have passed before us. The direction of the wind ceremony often celebrates Day of the Dead and related events, honoring families, and peoples in the global community. This spirit unites the water walkers, as Christina experienced.

I am moved by the passion that drove the Ojibwe people and their call for the protection of the lake. I think of the cruel history of Native American tribes and how it plays out every day of their lives. Living in communities deficient in primary resources rightfully moves a people to activism in a call for justice.

Christina explained, "I talk about 'tribes' because I know that term, but there are different Ojibwe troops, and they call them bands. On the days I was present at the Great Lakes two things happened. One was having the Water Walker Woman walk with the group on those days, and the second one was that the Walker Woman taught us how one person could make a big difference. It is said that she walked several different times around the lake."

In the Ojibwe ritual, women picked up a copper bucket and a staff, and they started walking. A young man accompanied the Water Walker. They were always cared for along the way. Every night someone housed them, and there may have been one night where the walkers were forced to stay out in the cold.

People responded by walking with her. She ended up having a contingent of people walking with her. We were all witnesses to the people's rights and justice related to water. I was honored to have been able to participate. It gave me hope to continue working in my community with women of all ages to strengthen their vision and commitment.

Another couple of Ojibwe people in our group did something called the Water Drum. They put it together while we were in a circle and the women in the group brought the water drum forward. The prophecy and the belief are that the people would be united again. I felt like I was in the presence of real historical action brought by the women of these different groups.

On Medellin Island, there's an area that's still a place where Ojibwe people can go. The rest of the island has been purchased, but they lease out the land on a 99-year basis. That lease is going to end soon. The tribes have to decide whether they're going to renew their contracts because it's income for the tribes. They may take their lands back and have this very sacred island that they call Ojibwe. There's a yellow flicker one sees on the island. It's a bird with beautiful yellow feathers. The place has that kind of magic to it, like my experience with the grandmothers there. So goes their prophecy, 'When the grandmothers speak the world will heal.'"

Lending a hand to important causes gives senior adults a way to stay connected to people with similar beliefs. Together they serve a common purpose. Many of the seniors I spoke with advocated strongly for their fundamental beliefs although for many, physical health limitations impeded their active participation as Corie, Anthony as well as Cristina and the water walkers have been able to do.

A different form of activism is Jaime's work, educating students and changing social policy in his writings. His work spans national and international boundaries. As an established sociologist and demographer, his work ends up in books and meeting rooms where he argues to include underrepresented students, like that of Corie, Anthony, and Christina, Jaime's work also reaches and educates the next generation.

Jaime says, "We don't realize how much our daily problems like the social services, wages from work, a government resource, and health plans involves public policies. When those policies get developed, officials call on folks like myself for the exact statistics to inform their policies. What I've tried to do is to describe the underrepresented groups through statistics on issues like educational policies involving university admissions, equal pay for equal work for low-wage workers, and benefits at the workplace. These are issues I write about in my policy papers and books.

I teach at the University of Illinois and work at the Institute of Government and Public Affairs, along with a part-time position in sociology. I focus on providing research to the legislature and state agencies. My work informs them about the demographics needs and policy implications for those communities. I didn't plan on working in this position. How I got to this position took many twists and turns. However, I'm happy to have had the opportunity to do my life's work with the many wonderful colleagues with whom I've worked over the years. We understand the bigger story of a people's history.

My parents played a big role in how my schooling and career unfolded. My parent helped to shape a strong foundation for me in an important way. Both of them were very pro-education, and my father had a very different plan for me. However, they didn't know how to advise me about my schooling. They had no idea how American higher education worked. Dad wanted me to work near home. Both of my parents had always worked. Dad was a factory worker, and my mom worked at a factory too.

During that time, televisions weighed hundreds of pounds. My father's job was to lift the television sets. They didn't have a belt, but the TVs were too heavy. His job was to lift them off the train and put them in boxes. He was super strong. He could lift 400 pounds and never complained. They both taught me strong work values, which I've carried into the future I wanted for myself.

My relationship with my siblings taught me the most about pursuing college. From the older one, I learned how to think about college. Then I learned how to help my younger ones. There are six of us, and although my brothers and sisters were very intelligent, they either didn't finish college or attended nursing school. Two of the girls went to nursing school. While I was at the University of Chicago, I came home every other weekend and tutored them in the math and science they needed to meet the minimum requirements for nursing school.

I didn't want to go to the University of Chicago because it had a reputation for being for privileged smart kids, academically it was kind of rigorous and very snooty, but I applied and I won the scholarship to attend there so I could live at home. I felt so very fortunate."

Jaime's account of his early life resonated with me, as did many similar stories of people reaching their dreams despite challenging situations. I'm hooked emotionally by these stories and remained fixated on how Jaime worked intensely in a career he loved into his later years.

"I wanted to study biology and go into pre-med. My mom encouraged me to do that. So that's why I was working with the monkeys. This job I had as an animal caretaker was intended for pre-med students. I could have gone to medical school, but you know one of the things about working in the hospital you learn, well, hospitals are not fun places. At the time it was a very high-pressure research institute, and I worked in the emergency room once. During the summer, I worked there as a volunteer, as an orderly. They had color-coded uniforms. Mine were gray scrubs. The nurse had blue or white. Doctors had blue surgical scrubs. The doctor comes up and talks to the nurse, and so he's like eighteen inches away from her and I'm also right next to the nurse and he says, 'Tell the orderly to go mop that up,' and I'm thinking that I'm the guy he should be talking to, and I'm visible. I wanted to scream at him, 'Hey, I'm here. I'm here.' I knew that wasn't the ladder I wanted to climb.

Then sociology entered my career path through a required core course. It was the coolest class I'd ever taken. I liked the subject of demography, so I don't regret changing. The University of Chicago had a dual-degrees option. So, I majored in Biology and Sociology. The money in sociology wasn't as good as medicine. I wouldn't even have to think about money if I wanted to become a medical doctor. Yet I've done quite well, and my family and I have enjoyed great opportunities to travel during my family's school vacations.

I' m pretty happy with my career in sociology and demography. At some point, the only thing that I'll probably stop doing is teaching. When I retire, I'll be ready to step aside and let those I've mentored step up and take over the classroom to the next generation."

Jaime's contribution to writings and policies put a human face on the Latinx demographic population in the United States. As Director of the Center on Democracy in Multiracial Society at the University of Illinois at Urbana-Champaign, he has increased the enrollment of

Latinx and African American students by twenty-five-percent.

"I'm a baby boomer, so in a few short years I'll retire. Since before college I've been doing some form of this work. I'm committed to working with underrepresented communities and recognizing the truth about that part of this country's history and the importance of policymakers understanding it. Policymakers need to be informed about underserved communities where many people of color live, which can help them to make the needed changes. It's everyone's responsibility to work for social justice in every way we can."

Jaime's work has significance for students, professors and researchers. Most importantly his written works influence the understanding of Latinx communities and its place in US for present time and future generations.

I'm felt inspired and impressed by one such community pillar. Kellie Duncan's story called my attention to the work that her loving hands created. Since she lived relatively nearby, the local news media's story about her work reached me through circumstances precluded me from meeting with her.

Kellie's handmade gifts for newborns were famous in Sacramento, California. The local hospitals appreciated her works. At the age of ninety-seven, Kellie had learned to knit. She served newborn babies in need of knitted caps and booties. At one-hundred-and-three years old, Kellie still worked on the project that had become her passion five years before. In those five years, she knitted over one hundred booties and caps for underserved newborn babies in her local hospitals.

Kellie impressed everyone with her gift and service. What caught my attention was the work of a ninety-seven year old person who taught herself a new skill for the explicit purpose of serving babies in need.

Whenever reporters wanted to feature Kellie's work, she requested that they show only a picture of one of the babies receiving and wearing her gifts. She deflected any attention to herself. However, in 2015, the Albert Einstein Center, a nonprofit organization in Sacramento, awarded its Heroes and Helping Hands Award to Kellie Duncan. With grace and humility, she accepted the award, saying, "I love the babies and knitting these booties and hats keeps me alive. I stay alive for those babies."

Just as the Curandera Cuca achieved safety for his community in her , the knowledge, skill, and wisdom of age abound in the service work that Corrie, Jaime, Christina and the Ojibwe, Anthony, and Kellie provide. There's no doubt that many have the potential and ability to be responsible servants in the service of others into their later years.

Their small and large contributions matter for the people in their settings. Senior adults often get cast simply as volunteers, keeping busy to avoid boredom and loneliness. Fortunately, many now reject the myth that age deters people's activism.[3] Elders who continue participating in the social change that's been a part of their life do so as an extension of their lives.

I've worked in communities where older adults from diverse cultural groups remained strongly connected to their social justice work in communities where they're engaged. These senior adults serve on nonprofit boards. They're community organizers, and they march in support of health rights. Some sing in local choirs and perform in local theatres. Some may prefer to do volunteer work in schools, hospitals, and safety net social organizations such as local food banks.

In spite of some difficulties, seniors navigate growing older with new skills and adapt to the changes common to this time of life.[4] To best describe this engagement of senior adults, I'll borrow the concept of Tikkum Olam[5] from the Jewish faith. In this context, Tikkun Olam connotes acts to repair and heal the world, and to support the welfare of society at large.

5

A Dollar Away

Seven older men formed a dance group called Los
Viejitos (older men). The group traveled around from
town to town, dancing with their canes. They wore baggy
old pants and jackets and silly looking hats with funny
little face masks that made them look even older. People
gathered around them. They loved the dances and
applauded for more. One of the Viejitos walked around
collecting money in his hat.

The Viejitos divided the money and moved onto
another street corner for more dancing. They all needed
the money to pay their bills. Some of them helped their
children to support their family. Raul, one of the viejitos,
had no one family and no home.

One evening Jose, one of the Viejito dancers, was
out with his daughter and grandchildren. They saw Raul
(one of the Viejitos) sleeping on a park bench. Jose asked
him why he was there, and Raul told him about not having

a family or money to rent a place. Raul's family invited him to stay with them until he could get a place to live.

Jose talked to the Viejito dance group and they planned a festival to raise money for him because many people knew of his viejito dance group. On the following Saturday, the Viejitos went to their usual places to dance and there was a big surprise for Raul at the last dance of the day. Jose gave a signal for a group of young children's dancers to begin dancing. Then an older group of children danced. The groups kept coming out to dance. At the end, Jose announced to everyone present that they had raised enough money to help Jose get a place to live. Jose was very grateful to his friends and all of his community. It was an evening of celebration. From that day on, Raul helped other people who also needed help because everyone had been very kind to him.

In the Martin family in a town near Denver, Colorado, the uncles enjoyed telling the story during the Sunday afternoon family time after the main meal. One uncle told the story mostly in English and sprinkled in a few words in Spanish. Numerous versions of viejito dancers' stories find their way into family story time throughout Mexican homes. An important message to the young people was the reminder that some people we know may need the basics that we take for granted. In the Martin family, the children said they were glad that Raul got help from his friends to pay for a place to live.

Financial security matters a great deal to older adults. Next to health, having sufficient funds provide for their needs throughout their senior years was the most important concern of the older adults with whom I've talked. Most people felt confident that having sufficient income would give them the ability to manage their health needs and to live in a safe neighborhood.

Older adults whose financial resources are ample enough that they can enjoy comfortable lifestyles in their senior years tell me that they appreciate being able to travel for leisure as their health and energy permit. They pursue entertainment interests, including annual season tickets for cultural events. Those who have adult children can support them financially to cover university costs and to help start their professional careers without sacrificing their own needs. Many people who enjoy these privileges see it as their responsibility to give back in their return to their communities and to causes by supporting them through philanthropy.

Some of the senior adults painted a very different picture in their life stories. Without financial means to care for themselves, some older adults must rely on family and other resources. Increasing numbers of seniors find themselves relying on outside sources for their survival. Where intergenerational family relationships are involved, treating older adults with respect and kindness at times becomes problematic when seniors rely on family members for their livelihood. And on the seniors' part, dependency raises mixed emotions, from love to anxiety and, in some particularly difficult situations, humiliation.

Whether or not they have family, many seniors have equally difficult problems when depending on meager monthly government support to assist them. Minimal income keeps some seniors financially fixed in the lowest income status.

Willie constantly felt trapped in survival decisions such as, "Do I pay for food or electricity this week?" Worrying continuously about these daily preoccupations raises the stress level for seniors. The consequences of his declining health relegated Willie to the growing statistic of low-income older adults.[1]

Willie expected to make it to retirement in his work. He said, "When I started having problems with arthritis, I really didn't know that it would end up like this. I thought that carrying the mailbag around town for many years had something to do with it. My wife and my one college-bound son had a modest life with me in this comfortable home. Then full-time care consumed much of their savings. I wasn't getting out of bed. Then I developed prostate cancer. With all of my health complications, I got weaker because of the pain. I spent most of my time being angry. I needed several surgeries because I had lots of things wrong with me. I've been from one type of therapy to another for over five years. I have all kinds of procedures I've been through, but when I go out, that's not the face I want to show anybody. I just quietly come home no matter how long it takes me. I've had this disease long enough to know that I put a lot of pressure on myself.

My wife got tired of caring for me. We faced hard times when I got ill until finally, she left me. The boys were older adolescents by then, and they decided to go with her. They didn't think they could take care of me. Of course, they couldn't. I knew that. They were young schoolboys. When she told me that, I didn't argue. I agreed with the boys. She said that she had given it her best effort. She couldn't do it anymore. I knew she wasn't happy because she began saying that even though she married me in sickness and health, I had become mostly sick and she felt quite tired. She didn't feel that she wanted to stay with me.

I knew that she was tired of being my nurse, but I, too, was tired of being ill and in pain. I knew that losing my job was due to my health. It had caused my wife a lot of stress. I thought our marriage was OK. She had a job. I figured we'd make it financially, but I had no idea that she was so miserable. It seems that she was pretty angry about it all because she felt ripped off. She took lots of our joint bank accounts and left me holding the bag. It was like she was paying herself for staying with me through hard times. She said that she needed more money because she had the boys. I got the debts and she got her freedom. She thought I'd skip out on support for two of the two younger boys."

By far, Willie isn't alone in becoming unemployed due to poor health. I felt a great deal of compassion for him. In my mind, I relived the financial hardship that I experienced during my health crisis and the career disruption at that time.

"Alone, every day I felt my life shrink a little more and it got farther away from me, "Willie said. "I spent more and more time alone. I knew it was unhealthy for me because I felt awful but couldn't push myself to do anything. I've just been trying to accept it all. I have little Social Security and a small disability pension, and I'm getting by somehow. How I know that I'm doing better is because I can buy both my meds and more food. No kidding, at first, I juggled it and wasn't sure where these shortages were taking me.

The shock was too much for me, especially since I had to move to a smaller apartment. My sons don't visit much, and I can't drive. When I want to see them, I have to take buses, and it's not easy for me."

Willie is not alone with his tribulations of declining health and financial assets in his senior years. This story brought back my own money troubles during a health crisis. Although my situation occurred while I was at the height of my academic career, I was only able to continue working by parlaying my skills differently. During the years of complicated health problems, my medical debts mounted to where I thought I'd have to file for bankruptcy. I don't exaggerate when I say that the weight of the financial burden sometimes had me relying on family and friends for groceries.

I'm grateful that my health improved, but as a senior, the threat of financial devastation due to a possible future health problem sometimes reappears. Ghosts from the past haunt us hard even while our scars are healing.

"It's been quite a while since I had to stop working and all the rest that happened. I'm still not used to being alone. I miss my kids. I missed what I had. I miss being with my family," Willie confided. "I have an old friend, Simon. One day he came by here because I live close to a little jazz bar in the neighborhood where he had begun playing. I'm sure he said that it was an easy enough stop for him to make because I must have looked pretty down. I barely gave him a handshake and he didn't know what else to tell me. He tried to kid with me and said that he bet me I couldn't play the saxophone like we both did when we jammed together. I laughed because the truth is, we weren't really good then, but we sure loved hanging and playing.

Well I took him up on his challenge, and I cleared the cobwebs from my sax and my head too, I guess. I started playing it alone until I felt good to see Simon again. It's a rough start with my sax. I still love it. I told Simon to pick me up, and I started going down to jam a bit. But it felt even better to play my music. I still miss lots of things. I miss working. When I had a job, I felt like I was doing something useful. I miss my kids. I miss our family life. We had a real home and real food. But I'm managing."

Being a senior in this society is a wondrous stage in life if seniors are economically comfortable and physically healthy. To make that a reality, older adults need equitable medical resources, proper food, an income, and a supportive social network. In the absence of economic security, facing poor health and isolation in later years becomes unbearable.

Poverty in the senior population has many faces.[2] Finding an exit from tribulations differs for families. Of the people I interviewed, a common thread is an important relationship that plays a central role, such as Simon did in Willie's life.

In Hope's early senior years, she became embroiled in most unexpected labyrinth of financial entanglements. Although poverty has declined among the elderly population over the past thirty years, the rate for elderly women remains almost twice as high as that for men.[3] In addition, elderly women are less likely to be married than elderly men and more likely to be widowed or divorced.

Hope's story is one of minimal lifetime earnings, the breakdown of the nuclear family, years spent in the low income labor force, lower likelihood of receiving pension income, and lower financial net worth.

"I'm nearing retirement age, and I'm desperate. I never imagined that at this age I would find myself in this unbelievable predicament. In some part of my dream, I'd be looking forward to working less and devoting most of my time to working in the community helping people organize for their housing rights and other social needs. Instead, here I am, divorced and six children to support without spousal or child support.

Last week I couldn't even pay the electric bill, and my family was in this dark house for over a week until I got enough money to pay it. In the evenings, my older girls went to study at the library until it closed, then took the bus home. I felt bad for them. I had the younger ones here with me, and they went with me to meetings in the evenings. I couldn't leave them alone in a dark house.

Only my oldest son works full time to help us financially, but he's been laid off. I've applied to every county agency to assist us, and that's how I stretch my paycheck and make ends meet. Every day I ask God to help us. I think it helps to at least not worry too much. That's faith. Some of my problems need answers that I would never figure out. Although we're being pressed hard from all sides, we won't be crushed. That's my prayer. When my children and I are in church, all of the burdens disappear.

In winter, when I most needed a car, it broke down when it began raining. As taxes had to be paid in that period, I found myself on the street, literally. I relied on public transportation until I saved up enough money to repair my old car. My family helped me so much as they took care of their bus schedules and got themselves where they needed to go because I had to go in a different direction to work. I learned the bus routes to my jobs and learned to walk the kids before, so I get on the bus for work.

I have three jobs to make enough to pay some bills. Neither one pays much. I make an hourly wage between $10.00-$15.00. I go to different jobs depending on the day of the week. For my work at the Senior Center, I can get there at 9:00 and be on time as long as the bus arrives on time. For my other jobs at the local community center, I can get there in the afternoon, and I leave to pick up the kids from school, take them to my work, where they can wait for me in the nearby park."

Even someone with a great deal of faith knows that there are no magical solutions to a problem. While Hope chronicled her events, I wondered how she would manage to turn her situation around. As much as she felt responsible for her family, she seemed to count on them for warmth and support. It seemed that Hope's family was a huge responsibility for her, but her relationships with the children were also a support to her.

"My sister loaned me her car for about a week when she didn't need it for work. While I had her car, I saved a bit of money, now I can repair my car. Now they tell me that it's not worth it fixing it. I need to buy another used car because I certainly can't afford a new one. It's like a juggling act with the family and not having the money to help them with what they need. The older girls in high school, who study and are serious students heading for college, have to take the bus.

Even with a car the hours are long. I'm up by five-thirty in the morning and begin getting ready. Then I wake all of my children who have to leave early. The two youngest boys hate waking up early. First, we all walk to the elementary school, which is about half an hour long. They eat breakfast at school. I try to talk with the teachers to get whatever report, so I know how they're doing academically.

My second oldest daughter is getting ready to graduate from school. Sometimes I have to go to talk to teachers or counselors. Since she's close to graduating, I want to make sure that she has all of her courses in place. She's applying to colleges, and she needs her paperwork in place.

My oldest daughter, who attends the community college, got a small part-time job at the department store.

Sometimes I don't see her until the next day. She was very smart with her money and managed to pay for some of her books and other needs. That helped me."

During the period without her car, Hope failed to pay a couple of house payments to the second mortgage loaner. Hope and her family lived in a modest three-bedroom house situated in a small, working-class residential town in unincorporated Alameda County in California. She had managed to hold on to the house for years since her divorce, but the last time she refinanced the mortgage, she got a variable loan. The payments increased, forcing her to continuously choose between paying utilities and mortgage payment.

Like the weeds after plentiful winter rains, Hope's mortgage problems grew. She was behind on her second mortgage payment. She received an unexpected letter of eviction from the loan agency that held her second mortgage. Her next step was bankruptcy.

"I was in trouble, and I didn't know how to handle it. I went to a minister that had been very helpful to me. I asked her for assistance, and she gave me the phone numbers of some country services and attorneys who might help me even if I couldn't pay their fee.

However, the attorney determined that the second mortgage office has been fraudulent in their handling of her loan and eviction. The attorney's efforts failed to reverse Hope's case. For all of his effort, the attorney was merely able to extend the eviction date for her family."

My phone conversations with Hope were constantly interrupted when her children needed her attention. She suggested a personal meeting. However, given the stress she was undergoing, I suggested that we reschedule. She said that it helped her to share this nightmare with someone besides those involved in it. We scheduled to meet an hour before she began working at the community center. It was a rainy day, so I thought the buses might be running late. I waited quite a while and texted her to confirm the meeting. No response. By then I was concerned for her, so I continued to wait. She arrived an hour later and was sincerely apologetic, "I apologize for keeping you waiting, but I was walking to the bus stop, and the sole of my shoe fell off. I didn't know what to do, so I took off my shoes and ran home. I'm wearing the only pair of shoes I have." She pointed down to her shoes. "This is the only way I could repair them." Hope had tied a rubber band around her broken shoe. I had no words. I just took out my wallet and handed her money for a new pair. She wouldn't accept it until I told her that those were her wheels until she got another car.

Eviction day arrived three months later in July. "I gathered all of my family in our home for the last time and told them again as I always had that we're hard pressed from every side, but not crushed. We were struck down, but not destroyed.' My kids were used to me talking to them in this way. The family had always been together through many tough times. Together we supported each other when their father left us. Whenever the electricity was turned off for over a week at a time, we laughed and cried through it. When my oldest son was in and out of the hospital because of his critical condition, all the family pitched in to help him. During the years when I was unemployed around Christmas time, there were no presents that year, but we had a loving time cooking our favorite foods. I always told my children that although life brought difficulties, the important thing was the family togetherness. We had each other, and I would make sure there was food on the table. This time the sobs were too loud for me to calm. We all cried and hugged each other. We had no idea when we'd see each other again because we're all scattered in different homes with friends who offered us a couch.

I took my three youngest children and stayed with a woman who offered her living room to us until I could find an apartment to rent. My two oldest daughters stayed with college friends who offered them a place. My oldest son also slept on a friend's couch."

Hope and her kids stayed in a friend's apartment, located twenty-five miles from her beloved community. The foreclosure on her house made every day burdensome because of the commute in public transportation.

"Occasionally, my oldest daughter loaned her the car when I didn't have classes. I managed all of this while looking for an affordable house. Every potential rental posed more obstacles for us. They wouldn't rent to families bigger than three children. Finally, I found a small home I could afford in an unsafe community several miles from my work and the children's school. I borrowed money from my brother-in-law to buy a used car. While I continued the dreadful commute to work and schools around the community, I searched for a place to rent in my neighborhood-the same place where I called home for over twenty years.

I know we can get through all the tough times right now as long as I remain hopeful. However, my biggest fear is that my younger children who still need me when I'm not able to work any longer because I feel more tired as I get older, they'll need someone to care for them. That's why I tell them to do the best they can in school so they can get to college and get a profession, not end up like me—old and working hard just to keep a roof over my family's head."

Hope had expected that her children be through with at least their high school education before her later years so that she could stop working and retire. She expected to have a job that would pay enough for her to retire. Instead she faced a situation far from her dream scenario. Hope had also expected to have a place her family could call home when she was gone.

Low wages, divorce, evictions, rising housing rates, and insufficient safety nets lead seniors spiraling into poverty. Hope fell victim to this trend that has increased among baby boomers in the past decade.[4] Like Hope's family, many seniors still find themselves in the workforce in dire financial situations, raising families and counting on education to change their children's future.

Although supportive relationships form the net that keeps struggling seniors from falling through the cracks, some situations compound the problems of family systems. When industries export companies abroad, they leave towns decimated. Unemployment becomes widespread when a company leaves. Suddenly, a workforce of thousands crowd into the employment office.

When major companies leave those towns and the town's economies deteriorate, seniors sink more deeply into poverty than younger workers, since they are unable to find employment as readily. This has happened in Flint Michigan, Youngstown, Ohio, Newton, Iowa, and Jamesville, Wisconsin, among others. While some towns have recovered economically better than others, Dave's story dramatizes the way late unemployment can impact one's life.

When the GM factory closed, Dave's world spiraled down to financial collapse. He discovered something he never expected-ageism. Companies that employ a large percentage of townspeople have closed and left families and entire communities devastated. Under these circumstances, older workers suffer tremendously when unemployed. This is not a phenomenon exclusive to Dave's story, but he tells how the fabric that bonds families and neighbors frays when the town's economy collapses.[5]

The GM factory jobs left Dayton, Ohio, and Dave along with hundreds of others fell into despair when they became unemployed. "I always planned on retiring in the position I had at the steel company. Good money. But when I lost my job, I didn't have any choice but to get busy looking for work, and the places kept shutting the door on me. After a long time, I was grateful to get a job in the parts section of GM. The biggest thing for me given my senior age right now is money. I always thought that I'd work till retirement to go comfortably with my family. Now I'm financially strapped. Throughout my life, I have always looked forward to birthdays and never felt afraid of aging. I didn't feel bad about turning 21, 30, 40, 50, 60, and now I'm closing in on 70. I've always wanted to work, didn't need to retire.[6] I don't feel old, just tired sometimes. I never said, 'Oh my God I'm getting old.' I've been happy about all of my birthdays. It beats the heck out of being on the other side of the dirt. You know what they say-I don't want to be pushing daisies. I would rather be on this side. I'm 68, and I'm glad I'm 68 because I want to live to 75 and 85 as my parents and grandparents did.

I hit the streets, looking for work. There are too few places around this small town that will employ older folk. So many of us were left unemployed. It took me a while to figure out that us older folks had positions at GM because we had been there for many, many years, since we were kids. We knew this town and all the business that had been there for years.

When the job search began to look grim, the depression bug got me down, and I couldn't get out of bed. I know I made it worse by hitting the bottle. That's not what my family expected of me. They're a religious family. I never had much need to go to church. But I sure felt that maybe I should stop in and talk to someone there. It was always my wife that pushed for that sort of thing, but I never felt like going with her and the boys.

I feel embarrassed that my boys saw me drunk. They were adolescents in high school. My wife raised them right. I didn't understand what was happening to me. I feel sorry that I failed them all.[7] I could see that my wife was very frustrated.

When I first lost my GM job in Dayton, my family was financially comfortable. It didn't take long to go through our savings without a regular paycheck. A couple of years afterwards my wife got tired of trying to help me to get out of my misery. Sure, we got a small severance check, but that would never last a lifetime without a job. My unemployment meant that the wife had to work to support us all. Everyone around here had a tough time. A buddy of mine said he's taken to cutting his own hair at home. His wife and the kids tell him where to cut, but they won't take to scissors. Got to cut expenses in any way you can.

Jobs around here pay only a bit more than minimum wage. She expected me to get serious about another job. When she didn't see the change she wanted, she got tired of putting up with me. What I didn't expect was the divorce. My wife didn't feel we'd ever get out of this sinking hole, so she wanted to leave the area and look for work someplace new. She took our two sons and went to live with her mother in a town on the other side of

Cleveland. She can have more opportunities for work around there."

I felt compassion for Dave's situation and the how his family was unraveling, but I also understood his wife's need for support as she tried to keep the family together emotionally and economically. Her salary was not enough for all of them. She needed someone to help her with the boys. Her future in the small town and the surrounding area near Dayton ended with Dave's unemployment.

"It took over two years of being alone to figure out things. I had to decide to stop drinking. A buddy knew my problem and was dealing with his own. He showed me where to go for help to face my demons. I hated it, but I knew I had to care for myself whatever it took.

At least my sons adjusted well with their mother. They're older and know how to care for themselves. Now I don't blame her for leaving, but I didn't think so then when I was left alone. Without my family I thought I'd go crazy. I was able to find one small job after another. I had to move into this very small, cheap apartment in Dayton. I spend most of my time here in my place after I get home from working small jobs that I got at the hardware store and other small stores.

When I visit my kids, I'm glad that they're doing fine with my wife at their grandmother's away from here. They're finishing school and have better job opportunities than I could provide for them here without my job. One of them is talking about going to college. I could never help them do that here. That's what matters to me.

As long as one has a job, I think that we can feel that we're contributing something. Maybe it's just being able to hold the board while somebody cuts it, giving someone a glass of water, but I have been able to make that contribution."

Dave made me realize that whether our work is as a factory worker or teacher, a significant part of it is feeling proud of what we do and produce. Beside his family, Dave's job gave him the meaning he needed. Sometimes we're oblivious to the importance of work until we're traumatized by a layoff, dismissal, retirement, or illness that changes that connection for us. Employment gives us personal meaning. I heard Dave express his new insight through the pain of stumbling to recover from losing control of his life.

"Alone, and no one to care for me, I began taking risks. I went from company to company to fill out applications for any employment that was comparable to what I had and even starting level jobs. The truth is that I didn't know what to apply for because the skills I had didn't fit any place in the area. People weren't making cars around here. So, I explained to the managers at the places where I applied for work that I had been a managing supervisor of operations for my unit. I told them that I knew how to show up on time and could supervise the quality of work of the employees. I told them that I was qualified for many different positions. I was willing to try whatever they had open. I was desperate.

I even tried to apply for the postal service clerk positions. They said that I couldn't work as fast as the people employed as clerks and that was the only position they had. I assured them that I was up to working at the speed required. They did promise that they'd keep my test in the file. Then one day one of those companies that held my application called me. They offered me a customer service manager position at a nearby manufacturing company for a year because the guy that had that position was on medical leave. It wasn't even half the pay I had before. That didn't bother me, but now I had a job but no family.

I began waking up and looking forward to putting together a plan. I think as long as we can keep feeling like we're working to contribute something, that's what life's about. It's not going to be the same forever. It's hard to change. It doesn't matter what it is. Without a job and poor health, you sink deep into the penniless pit, and alcohol will keep you there. I know of what I speak. More and more, I'm learning how things work around this town when someone like me tries to find a job. They don't like hiring old people no matter that you can work hard. I shouldn't be talking so much about how hard things are, but I never thought it would come to this.

I'm not kidding. Now that I have a new position has been the best thing ever. I was glad for the new purpose that gets me out of bed. I can get up now and have a cup of coffee with guys at the local small café. Just walking into a place where people know you and smile at you, it makes you feel like you're OK. We just sit for a quick coffee then, off to work I go. Feels good to say that. I'm recovering from the problem, and my world looks and feels very different than what I ever hoped. It doesn't matter that it isn't everything I thought it would be or might be at this point. I admit it. I went a long time hating that company and so did many of my friends. They left us high and dry. It doesn't help to know that other giant industries are doing the same thing in other parts of the country. We're all just trying to help each other figure out what's next. It's been tougher for some than others, but it's tough anyway."

Willie's, Hope's, and Dave's pointed stories about their financial strife describe the slippery slope that can lead seniors into a poverty cycle. Finding an exit is tougher in the later years. As in Willie and Dave's cases, in the absence of a biological family, friends, as well as other social networks, and jobs become like family because they constitute support systems.[8]

Successful coping with the absence or loss of the main provider in the family may involve adjusting traditional role orientations. If the head of household, woman, or man, departs as a result of separation or death, those left behind need to learn new ways of managing on their own.

Where finances may not present problems for seniors, other tensions challenge family relationships. Equal or greater duress for seniors occurs not only in their finances but in the absence of a family. Seniors living alone without a relative or friend to call on for warmth can find comfort in senior centers.

Veronica gets close up into urban poverty among seniors in Los Angeles, but her story illuminates the value of senior day centers anywhere. A gerontologist in the Los Angeles area. Veronica dedicates her life to older adults who do not have the support of others. She describes to me the daily needs of many whom she serves and the monotony she tries to enliven. Although women live longer than men, many men who live into their late senior years find themselves wanting to connect with others their age for companionship.

In her position as a Director of Service for Elders in Los Angeles County, Veronica cares for frail older adults of eighty and ninety years of age who live alone. Her clients are vibrant and engaged regardless of their physicality. Working with a population over eighty, she observes how their informal network shrinks each day.

A thirty-year demographic shift in the US has increased her work. Veronica explains, "I meet the seniors in their homes because I have to verify the personal data they report. I'm not a social worker, but I am close to the people. I have had the honor of working with people who survived the Holocaust, the killing fields of South East Asia, wars in different parts of the world, and they stand with positive attitudes. They love people, and they care about living in community. They're also some of the poorest people in our county. Hope for what their future will bring keeps them engaged even in small ways in spite of all they've survived. Their positive attitude reaffirms the human spirit of believing in something bigger than us."

Aging across the globe shows important trends. According to The United Nations, the rapid growth of the population ages sixty and older is predicted to grow by more than fifty percent in the developed nations. By the year 2050 that percentage will grow even higher for developing countries.[9] When seniors relocate to the US from other homelands, they often experience cultural conflicts in the process of integrating their traditional culture with that of their family. They encounter lifestyle differences since their grandchildren may not speak their language. A study of Chinese and Korean families shows that as seniors often find themselves isolated from the nuclear family, they are separate and live alone.[10] Many of these people are forced to find low-paying employment and to try to obtain Social Security Supplemental Income. Many also rely on emergency food pantries to support themselves in a labor market unfriendly to seniors, particularly to those who speak a language other than English.

"Many of the folks we work with are the last survivors in their family. They're alone without other people. Gone are the hugs, embraces and hands to hold. They've survived friends and family. Everybody close to them is gone. That's one of the realities they cope with daily. They wake up in the morning and have a bright attitude. In Los Angeles, a third of the older people live alone. On holidays like Thanksgiving Day, they have no one else other than our program volunteers who call them or make any contact with them. That tells me these are highly isolated older people. It reaffirms why we have to keep this work to support seniors in the country. We need to keep growing. For us, it also showed how vital daily contact is. You know America's holiday is Thanksgiving Day. It's about family getting together. For many of the clients, we see it's another lonely day. That keeps them isolated. It's complicated working with impoverished older people.

Some of the seniors attend senior centers and flourish with personal relationships they form with others. This help many mitigate the emptiness in which they live. Others, however, are too frail to leave home and do that. One thing that we've tried to do with seniors who have meager financial resources and cannot afford a phone is to teach them to learn technology. Technology offers an essential relationship for seniors in connecting with the world. It has also posed technological and financial frustration for seniors in these settings.

There's a commercial that I've seen where a senior woman says, 'I'm putting my pictures up on my wall,' and she thought it meant the wall in her house. In the commercial, the woman's children are telling her that's not how it works. That's the generation we work with through this office. When Facebook users say, 'I'm going to put my picture up on my wall,' one of our senior women did just that. She glued the pictures to her wall in her apartment, not understanding about the Facebook wall. I always describe seniors as the princess phone generation. People used phones with dials, and people waited for operators to answer the phone.

We're in the future now. I tell them that the operators of long ago don't exist anymore. Now it's menus and buttons and cell phones and all that. Some seniors are adopting technology quite rapidly, which is absorbing. We have some older people that are cell phone only users. That's cool. They have their smartphones. Some are learning to text if their eyesight is good. They have an active life. However, at least for right now we still have a significant group of seniors that need to feel confident with high tech. The absence of technology magnifies their feelings of isolation at their age and prevents access to resources."

Veronica's work to update seniors in technology hits close to home even for those of us who are not disabled. The blanket myth about seniors as non-consumers of technology is a broad generalization. Myths develop when others expect everyone to have the most advanced model of phones and computers when the latest model isn't necessary. I consider myself knowledgeable about the technology I use for my professional and personal business needs. My work requires me to use a relatively advanced level of computer operations. But as phones go, I'm not obsessed with having the latest model if my present model suits my needs.

Recently, I upgraded the cell phone memory. I also wanted a protective cover. With my upgraded phone in hand, I headed to the Sprint. I told the young woman who greeted me that I wanted a cover for my Samsung 8. She looked at my phone as if it was from the pre-industrial era and asked, "Wouldn't you rather update your phone?" I politely answered that while it was an older model, "To me it's new. I just upgraded the memory." Then she said, 'We only have one cover left." She handed me a case that required both hands to hold it. "It'll protect your screen too because they break easily. My mother has an older model like yours.' I just kept thinking about my dear friends, professors, writers and other professions who still function superbly well on their very early model phones."

Staying up to date with technology challenges seniors, particularly those who struggle with low incomes. Veronica describes how public offices such as the one she manages cares for frail seniors without anyone to get them to doctors' appointments. She's their lifeline for physical health as well as the emotional aspect of their life. Enabling seniors to network personally with others at senior centers gives them an opportunity to form relationships, which is vital to their well-being. However, when seniors are unable to leave their home, using technological resources assists their connections with others.

This country distributes resources unevenly. Some companies assist seniors from low-income groups with technological tools and the maintenance of the equipment. The older adults that Veronica works with live in what has come to be known as technology deserts. In larger cities, seniors find more available resources than in smaller towns. They have centers and libraries to access computers.

In recent decades, we've witnessed the extension of healthy life around much of the world. Older adults' capacity to continue working beyond the traditionally expected age for retiring or slowing down has extended possibilities for seniors. More remain active busy in the workforce away from home. Others work actively in the home without pay. In every place where seniors spend their later years with whomever they choose as companions, the most important longing is for dignity.

A question often heard from baby boomers and older adults is, how did I get to this age having worked all my life, and now I have to choose between getting groceries and paying utilities this week? The burden weighing on any one who faces the indignity when forced to decide whether to eat or pay bills is injustice. When speaking about their financial situation, these people described their hard work, despair, shame, anger, and strong hope in dealing with their shortages. These conditions compel the local, state, and federal governments to provide a just system to meet the financial and social needs of older adults with limited resources. In spite of the powerlessness that underlies poverty, seniors in these stories held hope above all else.

PART III

METAMORPHOSIS IN PERSONAL RELATIONSHIPS

6

THE GRACE OF SHOWING UP

In a small town near Hermit Peak, New Mexico there lived two children, Abby and Chitto. The two little ones found themselves all alone without anyone to care for them. They walked the streets every day looking for someone to help them. One day they saw a small wounded bird sitting on the ledge of their favorite store, which gave them candy and other treats sometimes. The small bird didn't have anyone to care for him either.

The children helped him heal his leg. The little bird was so grateful that he told Abby and Chitto that he would grant them a special wish for fixing his injured leg and helping him to fly again.

For their wish, the children asked the bird to give them parents and a home. The bird said that he had something better for them, a special surprise.

"Why are you bringing us to these old people's house?" The children asked.

"This is the Grandpa and Grandma Yazzie," said the small bird. "They'll be your parents and teach you many important things."

"Will they give us candy and cake to eat?"

"Even better, they'll love you and share their big family with you." The little bird told them.

"Wow, a big family with kids that we can play with?"

"Yes," the grandparents said. "They all come to visit us often. We all have lots of fun together and they'll love you too." Abby and Chitto smiled and told the bird that they would love to stay with Grandpa and Grandma Yazzie, but they wanted the little bird to live with them too. He assured them that they would be just fine with their new family and he would visit them often. They would be his little parents always since he didn't have any.

Abby and Chitto had a happy life with Grandpa and Grandpa Yazzie and all of their family. They ate great bread, eggs, buffalo, and rabbit along with fruits that they grew in their back yard. For celebrations, the children had yummy cake and candy too. Little bird visited them, and he brought his little bird family to meet Abby and Chitto, his parents who had healed his leg and helped him fly again.

Oftentimes, the Acuna family children in northern New Mexico requested grandparent stories. They loved their grandparents, who they couldn't see very often. The Sunday folk stories reminded them of how special grandparents were in their lives.

The children sat with all of their family after Sunday dinner to hear their uncle tell Pueblo stories. Since the uncle was a young boy, he had heard his parents tell Pueblo stories to the young people. Now it was his turn to gather the family and tell his favorite stories of Pueblo folklore.

In my earlier years, I spent a great deal of time with my grandparents, whom I loved. To this day, I think of my grandmother as the most loving person I've known. She let me pick out my favorite candy when we walked to the store and she would pick out a beautiful embroidered handkerchief to give to me. Grandma and

Grandpa played a major role as generous, kind, and wise cultural elders.

The experience and knowledge of grandparents are invaluable contributions in families. Grandmother and Grandfather were the stable figures for the young people. They were indispensable in keeping the community together. Such was the message that Margaret Mead advocated for by recognizing the knowledge that grandparents can share with younger people. When grandparents are called to parent their grandchildren, they help restore awareness that elements of the past move forward, which is something that protective services and foster care cannot do. In these families, grandparents build the bridge and they fit the role that Abby and Chitto's grandparents played.

The generational togetherness of seniors and youth is stronger than ever in the absence of parents, but grandparents' caring for grandchildren is not a new practice. My grandparents cared for my sisters and me in the summers in our early years. We helped them with the upkeep of their home and shopping errands. Later, when they grew older, and couldn't care for themselves, they lived with us.[1] Older and younger generations have always formed one family unit until the country's economic and social systems system caused families to separate. Nowadays, many occasions require grandparents to assume the role of parents.

Across the country, a growing number of grandparents have become main caregivers of their grandchildren. They've become a large growing demographic. The US Census estimates that there are almost three million households where grandparents are the primary caregivers.[2] Living some distance from their grandchildren makes it quite difficult for some grandparents but does not impede grandparents from playing an active role in raising their grandchildren with financial assistance and emotional support. Some grandchildren move in with their grandparents. Others' grandparents live in the home with the parents and grandchildren but assume most of the care.

Although intergenerational households often provide strong relationship bonding between children and grandparents, sometimes grandparents' needs go unmet when they are caring for grandchildren in the absence of parents.[3] They find that they're alone when searching for resources to care for themselves and their family unit that includes young grandchildren.

Sylvia's problem began when she left her home in New Mexico and moved to southern Texas to care for her three young grandchildren. Before that, she said, "I felt comfortable living alone, retired, and having a quiet life. Lisa, my daughter, and her family lived in Pharr, Texas, so I only visited them for Christmas and stayed several weeks with them to spend time with my grandchildren. At that time, they were young kids. Then one day my daughter called to tell me that my son-in-law had died very suddenly. I went out there to help her. She was very depressed and didn't know how she'd support the family and work. However, she had to keep working since they were always short of money. The kids were in school and had a rough time with their father gone. I stayed with them for a couple of months because I saw my daughter struggling, working, and caring for the kids. She was always tired.

Some weeks after I returned home, my daughter called me and said that she'd been to the doctor and they gave her bad news. She had developed stage four-breast cancer and they would begin chemotherapy very soon. She didn't have to ask me. I was on the next flight out. She told the children that she wasn't feeling well and that I'd be caring for them until she felt stronger.

Without my car to get around, I learned to drive my daughter's and figure out my way around the town. Thank goodness it's a small one, but it's different visiting the place and having to take care of the family. I felt I was working two full-time jobs. Everyone needed something every day, and my daughter was too weak to drive and had to get to the doctor all the time. I can't believe how quickly things went from bad to worse for my daughter. We never imagined that the cancer would progress since she was getting the most potent chemo, but she was getting weaker. We tried to prepare the children, and we called the priest to the house to help us talk with them. She got weaker every day and almost to the day that her husband had died the year before, I lost my daughter.

Her three kids were still in shock from the father, and now I was in charge of these very sad little angels. My grandson, little Lucas, was ten and the two girls, Jessica, and Emily, were a few years younger. Lucas wanted to take charge and help out with everything. I kept telling him that he just needed to be a good brother to the girls and do well in school, but I could see that he was always worried in his quiet way and always reminding his sisters of things to do and not do. He was such a responsible little guy. Sometimes I think he's keeping us all organized. One thing that even Lucas couldn't help me with and that was getting my apartment and things cleared out. I only had my brother, who can't lift heavy things. Neither he nor his sons are helpful when they're needed. I had to call the priest at my little church to see if he could get a couple of friends to help him clean out my place and send me boxes. I gave the church all my furniture to donate.

It's been several years since Lisa called me to come and help her with the family and so much has happened. I've tried to keep them on a regular schedule so that the kids get good meals to eat, go to school, and attend church on Sundays.[4] They don't like going to church much, but I tell them that when they're older and get married, they can decide for themselves. Lucas tries to support whatever I choose, but they're kids, and they get moody. I'm tired a lot, so I try not to argue with them.

The one time that things got bad was when Emily ran off with a friend, but we didn't know that till later at night. We didn't want to call the police till we called all her friends, and no one knew where she was. Then her friend Frida's mother called to tell us that she had found out that the girls might have gone to Frida's uncle's house. So, we waited to hear for sure before we got in the car. I felt very relieved when we heard something because the one thing that scared me was that our house is near a dump. That's where people dump old junky furniture and personal items when they leave town. I prayed quietly. I was afraid that she might have been kidnapped if she was out there alone or with friends.

Fortunately, she returned that night crying that she didn't like it here because I was strict. I told them that I loved them because they were my grandchildren and I might be old-fashioned to them, but I wanted them safe. The trouble was that Emily was also having problems at school and wanted to goof off instead of doing her homework. Lucas tried to help her, but she didn't want to pay attention. Between Lucas and me, we did the best to help her do better at school until she improved a little and settled down before she failed too many classes."

Several years passed since their grandmother began caring for them.[5] "Lucas was getting ready to graduate from high school and preparing to go to college. I've cared for them since Lucas was about ten years old and he's mostly a quiet boy, he has an incredible sense of responsibility and ambition the way he cares about his school work and helps his sisters with their work. When Lucas asked me to go to the school to talk with his teachers, they always had good reports. The girls did too, mostly they tried and were respectful, but he was always excellent. One day after school, I couldn't find him, and I went walking around the neighborhood nearby because even though he was old enough to drive, he didn't have a car. I asked one of the neighbors if she had seen him. She said that she had seen him and another friend walking around the back of the house by the junkyard. I call it. People who can't find jobs around here leave and dump their junk. I wasn't too worried about Lucas, but I asked Emily to go with me and check the back of the house. I couldn't believe what I saw. He was in the dump, reading from books he had found while his friend was looking for other things."

So much of Sylvia's story left me picturing the situations of the young family that she cared for over the years. Their family's resilience made me feel that a talk with Lucas would give the young person's perspective. Now as a high school graduate, his views of their early years with their grandmother would provide interesting details to their story.

Lucas tells about the years when Sylvia cared for them, "My sisters and I had a very tough time when our parents died because we were young and very sad for a long time. Grandma tried to keep us on track. You know, she made sure we got the church, cooked the meals, and she made sure we got to school. That's a big thing for her. I know she freaked when I was in the dump looking for books, but people throw out good stuff when they have to leave. I love to read science fiction, and books cost money. I've found lots of books down there. I also like engineering type books, so those I have to get at school.

I've done pretty good at school. I'll graduate this year with one full year of college credit and a full scholarship to the University of Texas, Pan American. That's a good thing because I can't afford to go without a scholarship. I still have to pay for my personal needs, so I have to work at least part-time. The university also offered me a job on campus, I'll live here at home and commute. My friends and I are fixing a car that I bought for one hundred dollars. Yeah, I know it's a crazy thing to believe, but it was a piece of junk, and my friends and I we're good at engineering and repairing mechanical stuff. We've rebuilt a computer for each of us. The computers were thrown out in the dump, which was actually our backyard. So, we're good at taking care of ourselves. The only difference for me is that I have to look after my sisters because I want them to have the same opportunities I had. This school district has changed quite a bit. Now there are so many opportunities for poor students that we didn't have before.

Today we're able to get into many advanced classes and begin college credits with the local community college. This way we have college credits before we begin university classes. Like me I'll have my bachelor's degree done in three years. Yes, it's been sad without Mom and Dad, I'm glad that Grandma was here to help out. I was barely ten years when Mom died, and I couldn't care for them so they told us that the County

Child Protective Services would have taken us to foster homes. I care for my sisters, and I think they've had a tough time without a real mom, so I can't leave them alone even if I'm in college. I plan to be here to make sure they're doing well in school."

Sylvia bridged the family continuity for Lucas and his sisters in spite of their adult and child differences. She felt it was her responsibility to continue the family practices. Grandparents are increasingly crucial in multigenerational families. Grandmothers may stress religious influence across the generations when living with them.[6]

Like Sylvia, Doug and Emma were shocked by the unexpected call. For them, the call came from protective services in the county where their daughter lived with her partner. "How do we explain to our dear grandchildren what was happening with their mother? We didn't even know everything. Protective services wouldn't let us have the children till several days after we knew that our daughter was in jail. They had to ensure that we were a safe home for them." Shocked, Doug and

Emma arrived at the protective services of a district on the opposite side of the county.

"The director and a police officer explained in vague terms that Susan and her partner had been picked up at their home because they may have been making meth and exposing her kids to illegal substances, and they found other drugs. We were never too pleased with her partner, but you can't tell Susan anything. We'd never imagined that something like this would happen. She's a grown person and has always been very responsible for Bobby and Jo, the kids. Susan came with the kids to visit us sometimes, and the kids stay overnight when they're doing whatever. We love having the children. They're a joy, and I've never seen anything that would make me worry about them. For sure, we never imagined that we would ever have to be full-time parents to them because of this problem.

However, the worst nightmare was upon us. It took days for us to calm the children down after taking the children to our apartment. There were so many questions about the charges that had no easy answers. The police wanted to question the children. They're nine and seven-years old, and we didn't permit it until we checked with our attorney. They were so young and traumatized as it was. We wanted to protect them as much as possible.

We split the time between settling the kids in school near us and showing up in court for Susan. It might sound mean, but we didn't feel responsible for the man she lived with. We made that clear to her. I couldn't explode the anger I felt about this mess because I wanted the kids to feel as calm as possible, and I was afraid that if I reacted angrily, it would make things worse for them. Sometimes during the day when they were in school, I let myself dissolve into tears of anger and upset that my daughter would get involved in something criminal. Then I worried how long she might have to remain in jail and the children would have to live with us. We just retired, and the kids need their mother and their home and friends. Now they were in a strange community and starting from scratch without their mother."

I first spoke with Emma over a year after the Susan episode. I could still feel the anxiety and exhaustion by the sound of her occasional sniffles I didn't press her on details about the case and let her share as much as was comfortable. She seemed especially preoccupied with her grandchildren.

"Probably the most challenging part of caring for my grandchildren is that I needed to cook so much, which meant lots more shopping than for Doug and me. I found myself preparing meal after meal. I wanted to make them the foods they liked. Jo and Bobby ate most foods, but meals were uncomfortable because they wanted an update all the time about their mom. We kept them informed with enough information as we felt was okay for them to know. It was important to talk about it because it wasn't a secret and the more they understood, the less anxious they'd be. Still, sometimes they'd break down crying when we talked because they missed their mom. It took several weeks before we were able to obtain permission for Susan to speak with Bobby and Jo. They weren't allowed to see her, but she could talk on the phone for a few minutes. When they did get to talk with her, it was the painful tears, and we had to do the emotional cleanup. If she called them on Saturdays, we'd take them out for a treat and drive to a museum or play area afterward.

It scared me thinking about all that went on in the house. I hope my poor grandchildren weren't contaminated. I've heard that kids can inhale fumes of toxic stuff and become addicted. Up to then, only Doug has been in touch with her because he got a lawyer for her and he was able to be present sometimes. I know she misses the kids very much, and I can imagine, and I feel terrible for the kids, but I'm still very angry with her.

My concern was the kids in school, so I tried to visit them in the classroom when I could. I didn't have the energy to volunteer as I did with Susan, but I needed to see for myself that they were adjusting as well as possible. It was a good school even if it was public. I spoke to the principal and the teachers and made them aware of the situation and told them that it was confidential. I didn't want the kids branded. Everything was difficult enough for them and for us too. The principal was very helpful. He suggested that they meet with the school counselor and I agreed. That's something I've considered for me too because life felt like it was in a fast freefall. We didn't see many friends because we were tired. Yes, we were always very tired, but we didn't want to answer all of their questions. My oldest son lived in another state, so he did call occasionally.

Dealing with an upside down family wasn't how I imagined spending my retirement time. We worked for so many years at the college. Doug was a financial specialist, and I was secretary for an academic department, and we were so ready to rest. Thank goodness we got a small pension, but we were watching the little nest egg we had shrink to a scary size."

I felt a sense of relief when Emma told me that Susan spent very little time in jail because she got a plea deal. I wanted to hear if the grandparents' relationship with the children continued afterward. Without a doubt, that relationship would continue, but it would change with Susan in the picture.

"Life got even more complicated when Susan was released. She had no job, no house, no money, and we had custody of her children until she could get her life together. Maybe it was a bittersweet situation that she had to live with us. We had Bobby and Jo, and we're her family so she didn't have to go to a half-way group home. We had so much work to do to repair the trust with her and her confidence in us, to be truthful. I was so exhausted that I didn't want to have to deal with her emotional problems. So, I let the kids go. It wasn't as hard for Doug, because he had let me do most of the emotional work with the kids. He loves them and all, but he dealt more with the court and Susan's legal stuff. I wanted to see how Susan would relate to the kids and make sure that she was a good mom like she always had been. The kids didn't want to leave her side, and I saw it as essential for them to bond again. I mean they could have been angry with her like I was, but they're kids, and she was a good mom. I felt okay caring for the house. It's a small and crowded place. I cooked some of the kids' favorites, spaghetti and meatballs and we took them all to a movie or a park.

Daytime gave me some respite and sometimes when Susan was home, and I tried to talk to her, awkward as it was. We talked about the kids, and they were our common ground for a while. She was on a strict schedule with her probation officer in addition to job-training sessions, counseling, drug rehab, and classes on raising children. Although it meant lots of exhausting chauffeuring between her meetings and the kids in school, I was glad that she was serious about turning her life around."

I somehow didn't think that I was through getting Emma's story. Something seemed missing. It didn't feel as if I had everything she could tell me about parenting for the second time. I asked her for permission for us to talk again. She said yes. The part of her story I felt was missing was her relationship with Susan. I thought it was a large part of her connection with her grandchildren.

Emma told me, "Countless counseling sessions under my belt gave me the strength and words to talk with Susan honestly about her feelings of what occurred and the emotional distance, as my counselor says, and be able to listen. She agreed to go on a drive, and we went to a quiet setting, and I told her that we needed to talk about her and how she felt since we had all been through so much. I didn't know how she would respond, but she burst into tears. I guess she had as many pent-up feelings as I had. I sat quietly and waited for her to begin with whatever she needed to say. 'I'm sorry,' she said. When I heard that, it almost felt like nothing had happened, that everything was fine. I had been waiting for her to understand the hell that she put us all through. I told her as much. She listened through her sniffles. I also wanted to know what happened to her and how she hid it so well from Doug and me. She talked about how embarrassed she felt through it and was afraid we'd take the kids if we knew and felt that she'd get out of it before we found out. It all backfired on her. I can't tell all of it because it's her private stuff, but I know that we opened the door to a more honest relationship. I didn't want to mistrust her, but I wanted assurance that we had turned the corner on this horror because the children needed a stable life and we're too old to continue this stressful situation. Doug and I just wanted a good relationship with her and the kids. We were even willing to get a larger house for all of us to live in, but these plans were not going to be part of the first talk or even the second or third. I frankly didn't know what it would take to be a trusting family again.

The most challenging thing for me to hear is what I might have done to contribute to her criminal behavior. I prided myself on being a good parent and couldn't imagine that Doug and I had any blame in her criminal behavior. I was willing to hear whatever her answer was to my question. She said that she was ashamed that we had been only good to her and her shame was all about her going against the values we taught her. She didn't blame the man she was with, but I can only guess that she let herself get swept into a scheme.

After many more conversations with the three of us, Doug, and us two, we began to speak of the future for all of us. First, we all had to get on the same page of what was best for Bobby and Jo. All I can say is that I feel twenty years older now than my real age. It felt like our family would never be the same."

Emma didn't speak about the importance of grandparents stepping in to perform the role that would otherwise get relegated to the county foster care system. That Susan's children were spared a long-term stay in the system was not lost on the children when they were able to get released to their grandparents who loved and cared for them in every way.

Until Zack's grandparents gave him a loving home to live, his troublesome path was leading him into problems with the police. Amanda and her husband supported Zack through this period. They loved him and wanted to see him succeed as they knew he was capable of doing.

"My stepdaughter and my step-grandson Zachary had lived with us until he was two years old. When they moved out, he remained close to my husband and me. He was the closest thing to a son that I've known because I didn't have children. During those years, my work kept me very busy, but I loved having him live with us.

We all lived together until he began school, and they got their own place. His mother worked, and Zach made their neighborhood his playground. We weren't aware of all the problems that Zach had because we weren't present all the time. Over the years, when we visited him, it became clear that he was struggling and very unhappy."

Zach's emotional problems escalated as did his medical issues. Amanda and her husband assisted him with medical care and helped him find a counselor, but he began hanging out with gangs, followed by troubles with the police. He was in and out of the penal institutions for a few years.

After his release, he went to live with Amanda and her husband. They mentored him and were happy to see him become interested in studying and succeeding in school.

"Near his senior year, he returned to live with his mom and continued studying. I was so proud of him. Zachary turned his life around and became an honor student in school. When he was 18, he was living with his mom and keeping up his studies. One evening he was going to meet some guy in Studio City and unfortunately there was some drug stakeout that was happening near the place where he was to meet his friend. The sheriff and the Los Angeles Police Department saw Zachary unsuspectedly drive into the scene. He didn't know they were police. The police didn't identify themselves. They thought he had driven too close to their car and might be involved. And, a federal agent shot Zachary.

Losing Zach was a very tragic experience for my stepdaughter and all of us. We've been dealing with that for the last four years," Amanda said. "There is a lawsuit against the authorities, and it's actually, going back to court because my stepdaughter won the lawsuit, but now the feds want to appeal it. Still, it's crushing for us because we lost him. We lost Zach."

Zach's death made Amanda more determined to care for her health by finding more balance between work and home life as she faces life in retirement.

Amanda feels grateful that financially she is somewhat comfortable. She has had a successful career as a senior vice president of Altamed Organization, a network of senior care programs serving the Southern California area, including Orange and Los Angeles Counties. Ample financial ability permitted her and her husband to care for family members while affording them recreation opportunities not possible for families without means.

"Retiring means that I get to spend more time with my husband and parents who need me much more now. I look forward to more time with my nieces and nephews. In the past, I've tended to work very long hours and travel a lot for my job, and I can stop that. I want to make my family the priority.

However, first of all, I need to maintain good health. That means eating right. I do that so that I look forward to continuing that pattern when I am retired. I've discontinued eating junk food or anything. When I was a child, I had a weight problem I was overweight into my, like from age six to twenty-two and up and down like a yo-yo. After that, I was able to lose the weight, and you know how I've changed my whole lifestyle and the kind of food I eat, so that has helped me now to be smaller because that is necessary for me maintaining my size being small. I want to be on the thin side I don't want to remain heavy because I was mocked as a child for that. One never forgets kids making fun of you when you are six or seven years old. I don't need that as an older adult. I'm not saying that I expect to look twenty years younger than my age I want to be healthy. Carrying lots of weight into our senior years is unhealthy.

Another thing I want to focus on during my retirement is to prepare myself for something that most of us don't usually want to think about, dying. I want time to reflect. We're Catholic. When he was alive, I used to talk to my grandson about my wanting more time to reflect on my faith when we attended church. Life has been good and the time to appreciate it often eludes us until it's too late.

Having my financial matters in order is important so that I don't leave my family with a financial burden. That's important to me. My husband and I have been cleaning out old files including shredding old checks and obsolete tax receipts. All that takes a long time and I don't want to have things in disarray and have people say, 'Oh my God look at how disorganized she was.'"

Countless reasons make it necessary for grandparents to parent the second time around. Courts consider the grandparents' age, health, and financial situation when assessing how well they can care for their grandchildren.[7] Sylvia, Emma, and Doug met the legal requirements of their states to parent their grandchildren.

These two families were more fortunate than other grandparents I spoke with who had met all of the legal requirements to obtain custody but were denied. Children wait and wait for their parents to return, and when the parents cannot return to them, the grandparents' place becomes their new home. Against the legal backdrop of bureaucracies, lawyers, protective services, and courts, grandchildren appreciate a family home rather than foster care homes. The pain of losing parents, for whatever reason, makes young people hang on to grandparents.

Familial unity provides more than a structure for young people at a time of need. It takes into account the strength and knowledge of seniors. Issues of health, economic, and social support may overwhelm older adults, and these magnify when they care for grandchildren. In spite of that, grandparents are valued for their emotional stability in supplying basic needs and experiences. Still, the new challenge may be overwhelming to grandparents in these situations. The work ahead lies for society at large to support seniors who have full care for their grandchildren.

7

ALCHEMY

The sun sets on the people near the small town of Bernal. It was a quiet place that housed many wild animals near the big mountain. The people did not fear any of the animals as much as the coyote. And after the sun disappeared, they could hear the coyote howl. They closed their gates to protect their chickens, goats, and other animals. The wizard of the town wandered the mountainside, making sure that the coyote didn't leave the mountain to find his food. He was a short man with long white hair who wore dark clothes and hid his hair under a floppy black hat. He was like the watchman of the area.

When the wizard sensed that the coyote was near, he turned himself into an animal. Sometimes it was a frog, other times a goat or raccoon. One night the wizard saw a perfectly round orange full moon light up the mountain and the town of Bernal. As a wild hare he went and sat by a small lake in the lower mountain side.

Oh good, here he comes, thought the hare. "Good evening, Mr. Coyote. How are you tonight?"

"I'm hungry as always. All the animals are hiding, but then I see you and I think that it'll be a good night for me."

"You may be right. It's a good night for good luck. I see something that I can't have but I know you can."

"What are you talking about, crazy hare?"

"See that shiny gold circle in the pond? It's a pot of gold and I can't reach it. Can you?"

"I know I can. And when I do, I'll keep all the gold," the coyote said.

The coyote dove into the pond and began screaming for help because he couldn't swim as he went deeper, trying to reach the pot of gold that was only the moon's reflection. The hare turned back into a wizard. Sitting away from the pond, the wizard laughed because he knew that he had fooled the coyote and kept the town safe on this full moonlit night.

Children in the Garcias' home always applauded when their father told this favorite wizard stories. The wizard possessed unexplained powers that made me wonder about the wizards and the illusions in our life.

I was an adult in my relationship with my father when I understood that the person I knew as the wild hare was actually a wizard.

As a young girl, my relationships with some adults were easier than others. My mother's gentleness mitigated Dad's sternness. On those walks with Mom on her errands, I saw a world that made me wonder how I fit in it. One sunny afternoon as Mom and I walked to the store, I noticed a woman wearing high heels, which had caught my attention before. I was intrigued that she seemed so tall, and yet she didn't fall. Tall women appeared like giants to this short, chubby five-year-old. I feared that if I grew tall, I wouldn't be able to balance myself and fall.

My curiosity about adulthood and aging continued. At the age of thirteen, I lived with my maternal grandmother for a short time. Her physical features intrigued me. She stood barely four feet tall. Her thin, silver gray hair reached below her waist. At night she unbraided it from the bun she wore on top of her head during the day. I wondered if my hair was going to turn silver like hers. How old would I be when it happens? Will it turn gray overnight? In my late teens, friends even two years older than me seemed old.

From parents and grandparents, I learned about being an adult. They were my first models of adulthood. My relationship with them laid the foundation for relationships that followed as well as my self-identity and feelings about family. I had helped to care for my grandparents in their later years while they lived with us. When they were in their 80s, I overheard many of their conversations with my parents before I was caught eavesdropping. They shared concerns about their family members' physical health. Their purpose in these conversations, I learned was about staying connected with family and friends and determining who might need a helping hand.

My parents ran an orderly and strictly disciplined home. They buried us in rules. My sisters and I were expected to respect them, acquiesce to their authority, and adhere to the rules. Mom and Dad engaged with us differently. Dad stayed emotionally distant. He was grumpy and tired from working all day in construction. One stern look from him made me quake. He was a man of few words who relied on Mom to be the mouthpiece between him and us. She voiced his wishes to us. "Your dad says...," was a familiar song around the house. Throughout most of my earlier years, I thought of him as an ill-tempered disciplinarian, and I avoided him as much as possible, except at dinner time with the family. He demanded silence during dinner. When he joked and was playful, part of me welcomed it while another part distrusted it. I merely smiled. Often, however, my little girl's eyes saw a grumpy Dad walk through the back door with his worker's black lunch pail, large enough for a coffee thermos. It felt as if Dad didn't know how to relate to women. Our family offered the perfect place for him to learn: five daughters and Mom were a real opportunity for dad to practice calm. However, Dad labored all day in the hot sun building homes, and when he returned home, patience eluded him. It wasn't until later years I understood that Dad's stern temper might have resulted from work-related stress. This realization would have to wait for its own time.

Mom was the gentle and warm adult in the family. She usually spoke to us with kind words, unless she saw us without a book in hand. Those encounters came with stern warnings to get busy. Her daily attire was impeccably clean, and on special occasions she was particular about her appearance. She had regular appointments to do her nails and get her hair tinted dark brown.

Mom's priority for my sisters and me was education. She gave me the first feminist counsel I recall hearing. Getting married is a choice. Having children is a choice. Taking your husband's name is a choice, but you better always keep your own checkbook. At first, I didn't understand what it all meant, but on a deep level this message remained with me. Being independent felt just fine to me.

Dad didn't share her choices for us. When I left for college, his displeasure about me going to a university that gave me a scholarship created a silent rift between us for months. Dad's life in Mexico had created his traditional attitude that after high school, women's roles were to marry and keep a good home and family.[1]

When our parents reached the later stage of life, their decision about how to involve us, their five daughters, surprised me. They refused help from all of my four sisters and me. Their departure from the Mexican tradition came unexpectedly because my parents were Mexican immigrants who had lived their lives close to their cultural values.[2]

In that tradition, children assume full responsibility for the care of parents. I had already seen my mother care for her parents for much of her life despite her own poor health yet when they needed help in their senior years, Mom and Dad diverged from this cultural belief and acted independently. By then both parents seemed in agreement. They encouraged all of us to complete our education. Mom insisted that we prepare for secure professions that didn't require us to work as hard as they had.

Mom and Dad respected my sisters' and my privacy once we had our families and careers. My parents continued navigating their life independently with little assistance from us until Mom became too ill to remain at home. She went to a nursing home for full-time care. There, Dad dutifully sat by her side for most of the day until visitor hours ended. He ensured that she received the necessary care to stay comfortable. My sisters and I assisted Mom in whatever she needed until her end. After a prolonged illness, Mom passed.

All the family rallied around Dad to plan Mom's funeral services. All the while I thought how unfair it was that my mother had died and we were left with an angry stranger whom I mostly remembered as saying, "No" during our early years.

Mom's funeral brought out the hundreds of family members and friends who loved her. A mound of stargazer lilies, pink carnations, and white roses covered her casket that rainy February morning in Los Angeles.

Early the following morning, I went to Dad's house to check on him. He had just returned from Mom's gravesite. I hugged him and asked how he was doing. He showed me a small cigar box that sat on the dining room table. Dad opened the box and unraveled a long white ribbon. He handed it to me and turned away. "To my beloved wife" were the words, in glitter on the ribbon that Dad had found at Mom's gravesite. He turned toward me and said, "All the flowers on top of your mom's gravesite had been cleared off because the cemetery mows down all the flowers weekly. The night of her funeral was the scheduled time for them to clear the grounds. The administration promised me that they would not touch your mother's site because she was buried just yesterday in the morning. They promised me that they would not remove her flowers," he repeated. "But when I arrived at your mom's gravesite, this ribbon was the only thing I found on the ground."

I was stunned to hear Dad's story. There was only one thing I managed to say, "Dad, I'm so sorry."

He added, "I was going to go to the administration office and raise hell with them. Then I thought, No. I can't do that because that's what I did her entire life. I tried to protect her and all of you, too. She's gone now, and I can't do that anymore." My entire childhood flashed before me as I realized that the person I'd thought of as such a difficult, complicated man was just Dad playing out his cultural role.

In tears, I returned to my sister's house and reported what had happened at Dad's.

"I always knew that," she said.

"Ok. Maybe this can be a new start with Dad."

Dad had found his freedom at my mother's disheveled grave in the cemetery.

From that point on, he began a new way of life for himself. Without Mom, he recreated his role as a father. He began new relationships with my sisters, something we'd never expected. Now eighty-years-old Dad discovered a new part of his life as father and grandfather. He called us frequently to talk about our work and families. On birthdays and anniversaries, he sent us Hallmark cards stuffed with a few dollars in cash. Mom's presence lived on all of his newly adopted practices. Dad stepped into her role as if it was the most natural thing for him.

Dad called us to talk. He shared stories about his early life in Chihuahua, Mexico. Listening to his stories humanized my memories of this man I'd experienced as ill-tempered during my childhood. He loved talking about his own childhood. Dad's first job was as a child of seven when he dropped out of first grade. He went to work in his uncle's grocery store, stocking shelves, cleaning and working the cashier. Dad had no choice. The Mexican revolution left a litter of dead soldiers on streets, making it impossible for children like him to get to school.

It was remarkable to see Dad at eighty-years-old transforming before our eyes as he must have done many times during his life. He now wanted to establish a relationship with his daughters as adults who had children of their own. We looked forward to conversations with him. One day he stunned me with a call to announce his decision to sell his house and move into senior apartments. When I caught my breath, I asked him if he wanted my sisters and me to visit some possible residences in his area. Dad's recent decisions broke with the Mexican cultural expectations that a widower may move in with a daughter after his spouse dies. He was explicit about not wanting to disrupt any of his daughters' lives. A senior apartment would be an easy solution as long as he was comfortable and living near his grandchildren.

Looking for a senior apartment with Dad gave us all an education. He had to decide how large a place he wanted. Did he want a parking space, or would he be selling his car? Did he want to pay for meals in the dining room with other residents or did he want to prepare meals in his mini kitchenette? After months of flights to Los Angeles to accompany Dad in his search for the right senior apartment in consultation with all of his daughters, he decided on an independent senior apartment, conveniently located near most of his grandchildren.

Following my mother's passing, Dad's metamorphosis taught me that we're never too old to change. It's possible to be 80 years old and remain open to change and growth in the face of adversities. Dad finally bridged the distance between himself and his family, whom he had raised in the United States where the language and culture were different from his. Forty years before, Dad was proud that when he crossed the US/Mexican border, he was legally and fully documented. He brought his wife and family into a new land. All of his daughters became successful in their respective careers.[3]

Before this point, part of me felt frightened by what the future might hold for Dad and all of us as a family. He freed me of many shadows and fears about what may lie ahead in my own older years. My fears had been colored by media and personal observations of older adults who either resist aging or live in austere situations where scarce resources complicate their lives. Dad's courage strengthened my hope for my own future. Being with him, I learned to restore my childhood curiosity, confidence, and wonderment about aging.

In his new independent senior apartment, Dad opened himself to forming new relationships with people from different cultures who spoke different languages. He spoke in English with people with whom he ate meals. Speaking in English with others was quite a departure for Dad, who had only spoken Spanish to Mom and us at home. He learned to live and interact with a different culture.

Two weeks after he moved into his independent senior apartment, I visited Dad. I ate meals with him and a group of three other men he had befriended. Dad introduced them as though they were long-time friends. One was a Japanese man who spoke less English than my father. Another man was a young senior, a former university professor who had retired early and wanted to downsize his life so he could enjoy traveling and leisure. A third man about my father's age seemed quieter. He did not speak. Dad, on the other hand, could not stop talking about the man in a wheelchair who wheeled himself up to the breakfast table. To dad, he was brave to be independent in his condition. He told me his own pains felt small after watching how some of the seniors managed to be so active in spite of being disabled.

Dad had been observing people's comings and goings in the few short days and could describe their daily activities in detail. After breakfast, Dad and I sat and he talked about other residents. "See the two women sitting together at that table?" he said. "They're sisters. Every day they eat breakfast and head for the library and join others in a group to talk about books. That's a beautiful part of this place. There are many books, " Dad said. "That older man sitting at the table across from us walks to St. Mary's Church every morning. I've seen him there on Sundays. It's too cold for me to go out to mass that early daily, but it's nice that he goes."

A while later in his apartment, he looked out the window and said, "I like that church across the street because they serve lunch to homeless people almost every day."

"It's an Episcopal church, Dad."

"They do important things," he said.

"Yes, they serve the neighbors."

It was a warm scene at Dad's senior residence. Throughout my early years at home, I never knew Dad to have friends who were not family members. Now in his senior residence, my eighty-two-year-old dad talked about his community like an anthropologist describing people in a new culture he had been studying. Dad's brave life-change taught me that new courage and resilience rekindle our older adult years. Looking ahead, I know senior years offer opportunities that I've yet to discover. I may have to learn to adjust to different settings, practice a different language, and open up to new relationships.

For five years after our mother died, we had a father, the man with a history who had been a stranger in my childhood. On a quiet Saturday morning, my phone rang. My father had been taken to the hospital with a massive heart attack.

My sister and I flew down to Los Angeles to join my other three sisters at my father's side. We all thanked his doctor and proceeded to walk into the room where Dad lay. Whenever I'd heard about someone being on a life support system, I had imagined one cord connecting the person's heart to a machine and respiratory machine.

Not Dad. Thirteen cords seemed to come out of part of his body and connect to beeping monitors that encircled him. Almost half the size of his former sturdy, rugged sun burnt self, Dad's face seemed sunken, through his hair was barely gray at the temples. I touched his hand gently as it rested on top of the bleached white sheets. The veins bulged out, making his fingers look bony.

I leaned down and kissed him on the forehead. "Hi Dad, I'm here," I said. "Carmen and I are here now. There's nothing for you to do but rest. Don't worry about anything."

My adrenaline propelled me so that I couldn't shed a tear. There was too much to do, too much to think about. Staying alert and strong seemed to be the thing to do, especially for those of my sisters who managed Dad's personal business. Within hours of our arrival, all five sisters gathered in a small waiting room outside of the critical care unit to discuss Dad's situation. It was then I realized why it was necessary not to fall apart in the midst of a crisis. In a solemn voice, Carmen informed us, "Dad's written instructions stated that he didn't want to be resuscitated, and we're bound by his orders to follow his wishes."

"What does that mean?"

"That means that we have to remove him from life supports," my sister Mary said. Her position as a critical care specialist in that same hospital made her the most knowledgeable of us all. She was the expert, advising us what to expect and how to interpret what the doctors were telling us. Mary suggested, "We'll meet with Dr. Grant tomorrow morning and convey the family wishes, and he can advise us on the process. He can tell us when the best time is for us to do it."

"There's nothing more to do now. Let's go home and try and get some rest," suggested Carmen.

At night I lay in bed, my eyes fixed on the ceiling, feeling again the empty powerlessness I'd felt during the day's events. Only the dim streetlight peeking through the window accompanied me. My prayers sounded unfamiliar. I found myself evoking my father's patron saint, the Virgen de Guadalupe.

It's me, Concha, Juan's daughter. Dad has had a great deal of faith in you. Whether he lives or dies, I don't want him to suffer. You've got to help my father through this tough time. I've only known him as Dad for a short time when he's not an angry person as I thought of him before. He's always been such a hard worker. He always wanted to care for his family. So, I need your strength to let him go and let you take care of him.

Only my sobs interrupted my pleas. As if I was watching a movie flashing in slow motion. I peeked into Dad's life. A poor young boy with torn white pants and an old faded long sleeved yellow shirt, herding goats, and sheep on one of his first jobs to support his mother and seven siblings. His Yaqui Indian heritage and the fact that he helped the family survive hungry days in his early years had formed Dad's resilient inner fervor. They lived in his grandfather's birthplace, Cerro Gordo, an indigenous community in the mountains of Durango.

The Mexican Revolution in Mexico and its violence and devastation had shaped Dad's life. Having to step over dead soldiers on the streets of Chihuahua had discouraged him from continuing school. Back then, battles between Pancho Villa and federal troops overpowered people's lives. Soldiers sometimes forced families to give up their food and water for them, and they forced families to shelter them at night. After the first grade, the young boy Juan had begun working for his uncle Pedro, who ran a small store.

Even at an early age, he looked for better opportunities to help his family. By the time he was eleven, in his third job, he sold bread on the streets and accompanied an old blind man whose stepfather made "pan ranchero." Dad had told us that it was delicious bread with lots of anise herb. He helped the man sell the bread on the streets on the outskirts of town. For this, he received ten pesos a month, which fed the family.

That same night, exhausted, after spending the long day in the hospital by Dad's bedside, I craved darkness and the comfort of a bed. Sleep passed over me, but my conversation with the Virgen accompanied me.

Virgen, I'm back. There was no change in Dad. I didn't know what to think anymore but talking to you helps me to remember who the man is that lies connected to thirteen life support lines.

My tears ebbed and flowed as Dad's story continued to play out in my mind. It was like watching an epic movie with many sequels.

At thirteen, Dad began what would be his life's career, working in construction as an alvañil (bricklayer). More than just setting one brick on top of another, Dad carefully mixed the compound to shape each red brick, then measured the exact number needed to build a wall, a fireplace, or an entire house. At the age of twenty, Dad moved his mother and younger siblings to Chihuahua in search of work. After they moved, the Gutierrez family asked him to go back to Jimenez and help them run the *empacadora de paja* (hay packing house). He occasionally returned.

Dad remembered, "In those days, the French were often millionaires in Mexico." He helped the French to build small houses in the sanctuary to sell furniture and household goods to Mexicans.

"You've left a trail of houses from the depths of Chihuahua to southern California, Dad," I once remarked.

Chihuahua meant not only more work opportunities for Dad. More importantly, he met Mom there. They were married in Chihuahua. Mom, who was loving, affectionate and sensitive, worked as a seamstress at the time. Within a few years, my sisters and I were born.

"The bosses were most helpful," Dad said. "They asked me what I needed when they knew that Carmen was born." Remembering, his eyes welled with tears of gratitude. "Just money," I answered. And they'd dig in their pockets and take all their money and hand it to me. He never even checked to see how much it was nor did they expected me to repay them." I, too, teared up as I've recalled dad's words.

We went back to the hospital for another day of long, watchful hours outside of dad's room until the night's stillness when I could talk to the Virgen de Guadalupe.

Virgen, Dad's challenges, and successes brought him to the biggest one, immigrating our family to the US to reunite with Mom's family. He had to learn a new language and deal with cultural differences while raising five daughters here.[4]

Dad had always been a perfectionist in his work. He knew less about living in the US than Mom did because she had lived here as a young girl with her parents and siblings, they were international migrants, working the crops. Later, at our home in Chihuahua, Mom brought us to visit all of her family. Dad always stayed behind. He had his company to run.

When our family immigrated, Dad faced tough times in starting over from the bottom up in his work. He knew more English than he spoke, and the construction job expected a fluent speaker. For that reason, they passed over Dad quite often.

In the 1960s, construction work paid well when he worked. However, underemployment was up to fifty percent annually, due to rain and prejudice in the union. Supporting a family of seven on a construction worker's salary required lots of faith! When it came to unemployment, shortages, or worries about making house payments, silence prevailed. My parents didn't have to tell my sisters and me when things were tough. Their silence said it all. I dreaded coming home after school and finding Dad's gray-blue Dodge parked in the driveway. It meant that he hadn't been called to work. Outside the screen door, I saw my mother's sullen face, holding deep her disquiet. Standing over the sink washing the day's dishes seem to distract her from the burden, which the adult part of me later understood. Dad sat in the room with her, looking out the window, his black metal lunch pail on top of the table next to him.

Dad's persistent conflicts with the bricklayer's labor union reduced his opportunities for work. When he needed our help at the union office, Carmen, my oldest sister, or I went along to help him. This office was located in the industrial center of Los Angeles. Inside the building was a huge dull beige hall, filled with men wearing khaki work pants. Some sat on wooden benches. Others stood, waiting, clutching their lunch pails. I remember it as though it was yesterday. Feeling people's eyes on us, I walked close to my father, his strong Yaqui Indian presence calling attention to us. My father approached the desk where the face of prejudice sat. I looked at the woman behind the counter while my father said to me "*Diles que ya estoy arto de todas las mentiras. Yo sé que me rechasan a mi y le dan el trabajo a otros porque lo veo.*" (Tell them that I'm tired of all their lies. I know that they keep rejecting me and giving work to others because I see them doing it.) I relayed the message. My dad and the woman flung grating words at each other with a venom that frightened me. The argument crescendoed until my father walked sternly toward the door, and I followed.

At first, I felt embarrassment sink in the pit of my stomach, like the first day of school, when every eye in the room rested on me. His anger scared me as much as the thought of not having enough money. Most children don't see these rage outbursts. I hadn't. On this one trip, I understood. It embarrassed me when he shouted at the people in the office, but his frustration at being discriminated again so that he couldn't work must have been even more painful. That much Dad understood.

I didn't like to be absent from school. I dressed as though I was going to class in case Dad had time to drive me to school. In the car, Dad talked aloud telling me, "Pay attention to this system. It's cruel! Unjust!" I couldn't get Dad's argument with the people at the union out of my mind. My heart ached to hear Dad say that even trying to work in this cruel system. It was my earliest lesson in the meaning of social justice. Lord knows, these words meant little to me at the time, but my understanding of social justice deepened over time. Dad challenged and questioned how the system worked until he understood it so that he could have more control of his situation. He asked lots of questions, stayed informed and helped us, his daughters, to do the same. I always remember that about him.

My night of remembering passed. The next morning, my sisters and I walked into the hospital with our coffee for another day in the critical care unit where Dad lay on life support. We kept vigil while the doctors waited for the decisive moment, the right moment, the right moment to remove Dad from the machines and allow him to die with dignity. Hour after hour, we sat on the floor, propped against the wall in the hallway outside his room.

Sharing stories about each other and Dad kept our spirits up and munching on chocolate truffles kept our adrenaline going. Whenever one of us took a break outside the hospital, our bag of assorted chocolates was replenished. Noticeably, no one ever brought fruit or anything healthy. Stress doesn't always bring out the sensible part of us.

This day, I couldn't wait for nighttime to talk with the Virgen de Guadalupe. While visiting Dad in his room, I continued my petition.

Virgen, there's no change in Dad. He's in your hands. We're all certainly willing to help him in whatever way is necessary if you deem that he should return to us. But it's his journey, and it's up to you. Walk with him on his road. His life story has demonstrated courage, hard work and endless faith in you.

During our early years at home, I watched Dad paint our house many times. When he painted, he became an artist. He wore a funny white round cap that fit tight, like a skullcap. Only his ears protruded. His long white butcher apron and white gloves covered him completely, as he blended into the canvas that covered every inch of the floor from wall to wall. In between his meticulous strokes, Dad would step back, hold his brush upwards, and look around for approval from us. "*¿Qué te parece?*" (What do you think?) He'd ask. There was only one thing we could say, "Wow! Very nice, Dad." Then he proceeded to point out how he had painted the entire wall without as much as one drop of paint on the canvas covering the floor. Around every corner of the house he posted caution signs. We watched our every step and cleared the house until dinner time.

Dad had been obsessed with cleanliness, simplicity, and perfection in every detail of his life. His possessiveness about his work tools symbolized his identity with hard work and his need to always do things right.

I remembered that tending his vegetable garden had delighted Dad. A neatly manicured yard was equally important to him. The first house my parents purchased was a small house with a backyard three times its size and more than ten fruit trees. Dad expected us to help him clean up the yard, and one autumn when we didn't do our share, he took drastic measures to make my sisters and me help clean it up. He walked out from the garage with a hatchet in hand. I held my breath as he swung the ax at the first peach tree, and I felt guilty for not raking the leaves. My sisters and I stood behind the thin kitchen screen door, watching Dad whack down the plum and apricot trees to half their size. I felt each blow, wondering if the trees knew how brutal their fall would be this year! Afterward, Dad handed us Hefty plastic bags, and we quietly stuffed them full of leaves.

For someone who resisted change, Dad always summoned up the courage to learn a new way to do things. Coming to the US meant starting over as a bricklayer and leaving his contractor company, which he had organized. Whether it was learning a new job, a new language, or a new culture he accepted the challenge.

Back in the hospital, Dad's doctors continued to keep us informed. As Dad lay there immobile, I wondered what life lessons he was learning. Not that he would be analyzing his life cognitively, but in the spiritual sense.

Nighttime didn't come fast enough for me. My thoughts tumbled around. I knew he was tired. He'd told my sisters and me that for some time. I'd heard him say that growing older and frail would make him dependent on us. With all my heart, I wanted what was best for him.

Virgen, please know that he is not a burden to us even when he gets pretty stubborn because he's such a headstrong guy.

"One cent could get you a cup of goat's milk when I delivered it," I remembered Day saying. "I was about ten years of age then. My friend and I rode separate burros to get the goat's milk up the mountainside. It took us about half an hour to get to that mountain. The problem was that we had to arrive by 5:00 a.m. so that the people could start their day with fresh milk. One Sunday morning we rode off as usual, but it had been raining, and when we were up in the mountain roads, the burros started slipping and dancing around in the mud. We tried hard to hold onto our jugs from falling. But we couldn't stop the jugs from spilling when the burros fell and knocked us off. 'Oh no!' my friend shouted. 'Our milk! Now we have to go home without any money.' My mother counted on that money to feed the family and here

I showed up all muddy without any money. We just headed back up to the mountainside to start milking goats again and praying that the burros wouldn't slip." Dad's laughter was contagious, and soon we were all laughing. He had a way of making humor of his misfortune, so that reminiscence always ended with a humorous twist.

Virgen, even when Dad and I had conflicts, he managed to concern himself with my safety. 'How's your car?' he'd say. Then Dad would take the car out to fill it with gas. Sometimes he returned my car with four new tires.

The doctors told us that Dad was not truly alive any longer. "It's been five days, and we've done everything possible. It's time to let him pass on with dignity," the doctor said.

My sisters and I gathered and made peace in our respective faiths. One doctor instructed the nurse to come in. "Your father has been on quite a bit of sedation, and he's not in any pain," the doctor assured us as he approached Dad's bed.

First, they removed the breathing tube, followed by the cords connecting Dad to other monitors. When they had removed all of the lifelines that kept his organs artificially functioning, my sisters and I gathered around the bed and watched in shock as Dad opened his eyes wide and looked straight at the doctor near his head. In a thick, hoarse, and scratchy voice, with a Spanish accent, Dad asked, "What happened?" We gasped. The doctor half smiled, then frowned and looked at me, so pale that I thought he might need to be resuscitated. He walked over toward me, saying, "This is nothing short of a miracle. I've never seen this happen." By then we all rushed to Dad's side, telling him not to be afraid, that everything was fine and that he needed lots of rest. We had no way of knowing what would happen next. We held his hand and stroked his hair and told him to rest. He wiggled and squirmed, wincing with pain, but his words were mumbled, unlike his question to the doctor.

The doctor took us aside and told us that he had no way of knowing how Dad would manage through the night, but he suggested that we let him rest and try to orient himself. We went home. That was the first night since Dad first went on life supports that I got any sleep. Except for thanking the Virgen de Guadalupe, I didn't pray much. The phone didn't ring that entire night, and as day broke, the future of Dad's condition remained a mystery.

To ease my worry, I called the hospital, but no one in the critical care unit could provide any information because they were in the midst of a changing staff. My sister picked me up after breakfast. In the hospital, Dad had disappeared from his room. Anxious, I ran to the nurse's desk. "Let me check," the attending nurse said.

"He was moved to the cardiac unit on the second floor. One floor down directly under this unit."

My sisters and I ran down to Dad's room. There he was, sitting up in bed without a single tube or cord attached to him, laughing at *I Love Lucy* on TV while sipping a thick, coffee-flavored liquid through a straw. He lit up when he saw us. He laughed and laughed. His voice was still raspy and some of his words were incomprehensible. He didn't have a clue that he had been on life support for five days. When he finished watching his TV episode, my sister asked him, "So, Dad where were you?" I found this a curious question, but she was intent on finding out what "near death" story Dad would tell. We huddled close to his face to hear every word he had to say.

"I don't know what happened, but the last thing I remember is that I was with your mom, driving to Las Vegas. She wanted to go. And we got there and went into a big, big casino. The light was really bright. It was so bright that it almost blinded me. Then your mom said that she had to go to another part of the building and told me to wait there for her because she'd return for me. I waited and waited, but she didn't come back." Dad began to whimper. "So, I had to come home by myself. That's all I remember." I put my arm around his back, and my sister held his hand.

I looked at my sister and said, "You've got to admit, it's the most original version of the walking to the light story you've ever heard. The stories that I've heard are usually of people going through some dark tunnel to follow the light, but Dad went to Las Vegas."

With each passing day, Dad got stronger. After spending only two days in the cardiac unit, he was moved to a rehabilitation nursing home. It was the same facility where Mom spent the last two months of her life, near his home. More than the physical strength that Dad recovered, it was his unconditional commitment to life that amazed us. His loving manner, sense of humor, and jovial attitude about his situation made visits with him easy-going and pleasant. He showed true gratitude for the nursing staff that helped him in physical therapy and to get around on his walker. Both of these activities meant that others had to touch him, and Dad had to be dependent on them. Whereas before he detested being touched, he now welcomed it.

One outcome of Dad's stay in the nursing home was his friendship with Sammy who shared the room with him. Dad, had spent his life relishing solitude, now he reached out to Sammy. Both Mexican and Spanish-speaking men enjoyed each other's friendship and conversations. In this setting, Dad fully embraced life in a patient and loving way. He had resisted many grueling transitions throughout his life with equal intensity. Now he surrendered to living calmly, with gratitude, open to love from everyone around him and his new companion, Sammy.

Nothing seemed as important to me as spending time with Dad as he recovered step by step. I traveled down to Los Angeles to see him on weekends, and during the week I called him every night. Every time he had a new inspiring story of how he was feeling stronger, eating steak, and visiting with the countless family members that went to see him. He asked me about my work. I shared with him the exciting highlights of my upcoming trip. During that period, I was preparing to travel to Philadelphia to deliver a keynote address, and every night I updated him.

His memory got increasingly sharper, as I observed through his questions. "Philadelphia, that's in Pennsylvania isn't it?"

"Yes, Dad," I answered, "and it's freezing back there now."

"You better dress warm," he warned.

Following my trip, I called Dad just before they delivered his dinner tray. "How was your trip?" he asked. I told him that my presentation was successful. He had to use the hall phone because the one near his bed did not work. Dad surprised me. He was able to stand up on his own. I applauded him for being so courageous and making an effort to get stronger. They say that you're going back to your apartment tomorrow, Dad.

"We'll see," he answered.

"Dad, if you don't feel ready to go home, you can wait. No need to rush this."

Then I mentioned that I had to get someone to prune my lemon tree because it was growing out of control.

"Yes, you need to start at the top and cut it all back. All the way to the bottom," he said.

I had a flashback to when he chopped down all of our twelve fruit trees because we didn't help him rake leaves.

Dad said, "No, don't cut the lemon tree. Just cut back the overgrowth."

"Ok, Dad." Then he said that he was tired. I told him that I loved him, and we hung up.

Three hours later, my sister Mary called from the hospital, "Dad had a heart attack. Right now, they're just keeping him comfortable. I'm sure you know that if he had a heart attack this time, they would not resuscitate." I sobbed uncontrollably. Dad's voice still rang in my ears, telling me how to prune my lemon tree.

"The sisters and husband are here, but Dad is still conscious, and he's asked for all of the grandchildren to come."

"I'll pray for him."

In my deep meditation, I drifted off to sleep. In the dream, a young Dad carried a bouquet of deep red roses to place at the shrine of the Virgen de Guadalupe. I had a peaceful feeling until the phone rang.

"He's gone," my sister said softly. "He did it his way. In the end, he gathered us all around him and took off his oxygen mask. He prayed with us and told us that he loved us. Then he said, 'I have to go. Your mom is waiting for me.'"

I couldn't respond. I cried uncontrollably, choking on my tears.

My sister Lucy reported that during that week he kept saying that he was going home. And when she assured him that he would go back to his apartment if the doctor released him, he told her that he was going to his big home to see Mom.

When his time arrived, I'm told that Dad called across the room to Sammy, his new found friend. He said to him that he was dying. Sammy called the nurse, and together they began praying together to the Virgen de Guadalupe.

The hard-working young boy who herded goats and later owned his construction company grew up to have his own family whom he cared for till his last day. This man who had cherished solitude in his later years opened his heart to foster loving relationships with his family and even make a good friend before leaving. He miraculously recovered after a week on life support. Most of all, I miss his laughter, his opening Christmas presents with his grandchildren, teaching us how to read the world, tending to a neat garden and enjoying tortillas and rice and beans.

Hundreds of family and friends attended Dad's funeral. Family members talked about how they knew Dad to be a hard worker when he did jobs for them in their homes. People from his retirement home called him "a real gentleman." We felt proud to be his daughters. He had made many friends, and mostly he had he gotten to know his daughters and grandchildren. I believe we had an intelligent and responsible father all of our early years at home and a great dad for the last years of his life.

Dad was laid to rest next to Mom. We made clear to the cemetery administration that his flowers must not be removed from his gravesite, as they had done after Mom's funeral. All of his daughters made sure that his wishes were respected.

In several years, I'll reach the older adult stage that my parents were at the ends of their lives. Although my experiences have been markedly different from my parents', my relationship with them continues to influence this chapter of my life. Dad's later years taught me that it's never too late to change the important matters in my life. I most appreciate this the man whose authoritarian presence I fought from my early years to adulthood. I had the privilege of making him my best friend in his later years.

PART 1V

OBSERVATIONS

8

REFLECTIONS

A long time ago, in a village far, far away, people were friendly. They worked, loved their families, and went to church. The village people feared only one thing, the soldiers. They were mean men. They imprisoned people when they found them in church. Over the many years of enduring the threat and injustice from the soldiers, many people fled the village. They waited for darkness and quietly left for safer cities. Sometimes they left for country.

People in this village stopped meeting at church. They began gathering in a different building with a big basement. One day, just before darkness, many families met there. It was their place to pray and to visit with their friends while the children played with each other. The soldiers swept in on horses and found them. They rounded up all of the men. Then they went door to door and arrested the men who were home. The women and children were left all alone. Without work, they families lost everything they had.

One day, the Firebird came to the village and told the women and children to get ready to go to the jail to release their husbands and fathers. The women knew of the Firebird, but they had never seen it because it hid and only appeared when people needed help. The Firebird was a magical character. Its wings were of many different bright colors of red, blue, green and gold. It lit up the sky like a full moon.

The Firebird waited until all of the guards were asleep, then lit the sky to guide the women on their way to the jail. The women were prepared with instruments and the children carried bags of belongings. The women and children arrived quietly, and soon the men were freed. The Firebird led the families out of the village to live in a safe city.

After that night, the people never saw the Firebird again.

The Firebird lived strong in grandfather Koval's heart. The Koval family gathered late Saturday afternoons and listened to the grandfather tell folk stories with characters from old myths. The fact that the Koval family had refugee status in the US from Russia as did the community where they lived explains the theme of the Firebird story that grandfather told. Although the children spoke English very well, the adults in the family took a bit longer to speak English. The family preferred to speak Russian at home, and during story time, Grandfather told his stories in Russian.

My personal story has been a reversal of the usual pattern. I've lived through a life-threatening, autoimmune illness since a much earlier age, including years spent in a wheelchair. In my early middle-age, I remember thinking that I knew what it felt like to be a ninety-year old in a fragile condition. Through a very active role on my part to heal myself, I managed the autoimmune illness and have become healthier as I have grown older. From this vantage point, I can understand older adult health problems with great a deal of empathy. I'm aware of the possible health difficulties that may occur in this phase of my life as I enter my senior years, I have become quite aware of comments that seniors make about the onset of pain and discomfort along with chronic health problems. Having been assertively engaged in my healing I'm aware of the need for us to stay informed and involved when addressing health concerns. These senior adults' life stories kept this notion present in my mind.

One word I had expected to hear more often throughout the life stories is "wisdom." Yet listening to each person, I felt that his or her relationships were founded on wisdom. The relationships that they shared with me spoke of strife, laughter, tears, joys, and active intellect. Two older adults that embodied wisdom to me have shadowed me throughout my journey in writing this book. All the time that I spent with these two special older women left a memorable impression on me. This imprint has sustained my vision of qualities and of the inspiration that enlivens me now, in this stage of my life. One was my maternal grandmother, Trini. The other one was my husband's Aunt Gail.

During a summer vacation visit from college to my parents, my mother filled in grandmother's story that I hadn't heard before. She had married at the age of sixteen in Mexico, and had twelve children, of which eight lived. The family made their home in Mexico during the time they were international agricultural workers. When that period ended, my grandparents and most of the family remained in the US except for my mother, who stayed in Mexico. There she married and had my sisters and me.

When our family immigrated to Los Angeles, I spent my early years with Grandma. I've always thought of her as the most loving person I've ever known. I lived with her on and off through my childhood up to the time I left to go to the University of the Pacific for my undergraduate degree. Summers with Grandma, who was in her seventies then were wonderful early years. I loved spending time with her. She and Grandpa did not own a television. I helped to clean their house and do small chores. Every morning I walked into the kitchen where she waited for me with a hot cup of *café con leche* (coffee with hot milk), a piece of *pan dulce* (Mexican sweet bread), a warm hug and a kiss on the cheek. She sat with me to talk. Grandma wasn't much of a conversationalist, but she cared if I slept comfortably and she reminisced a bit about my uncles when they were young. She always had a kind word for and about everyone. Then she invited me out to her backyard garden where she kept rows of potted flowers, from geraniums to daisies and every variety of cacti and succulents. She showed me how to clear the weeds around the pots and water them, just a small trickle every few days. On her longer errands, Grandma would invite me to walk with her to the department store a few blocks away. She'd always buy a small gift for me. Usually it was a handkerchief embroidered with pink and yellow flowers like those in her flower pots at home.

When Grandma was in her eighties, she pinned her long silver hair up in a bun. On Sunday mornings her gentle voice greeted my family and me when we picked up my grandfather and her for church. When we returned to their little three room house, she prepared beans, Mexican rice, and a couple of chickens with a stack of corn tortillas for lunch to satisfy our family as well as the uncles and cousins who had arrived by then. She had a hug and a kiss for everyone who visited along with an invitation to the kitchen for one of her signature meals.

When they were in their nineties, Grandma and Grandpa moved to our house to live with us so that we could help care for them. When she needed help walking across the room, our grandmother in her loving way asked one of us to assist her. I only spent a year with them before I left for college, but I'm grateful to have had the opportunity to spend time with a frail grandmother doing her best to help my mother in their care for Grandpa.

Aunt Gail came into my life because she was my husband's aunt. She was ninety-five when we visited her in her senior apartment in Minneapolis. She had lost much of her eyesight. Her small, one-bedroom apartment was in an assistant living facility making independent living safe.

When we arrived, she let us into her apartment. She had a watch that informed her where to be at any given time. Aunt Gail greeted us with a big hug and kiss. She had just returned from the farmer's market, where she had bought basil, walnuts, parmesan cheese, olive oil, garlic and lemon. These were all of the ingredients for her pesto. Gail explained that she was experimenting with a new recipe, which she heard on the cooking channel. It included walnuts instead of pine nuts. She asked that we walk with her to her garden in the back lot of the apartments. Each resident had a small plot on which she could plant anything she wished. Her garden patch looked like the corn fields of Iowa, where she had spent much of her life. The large, red, plump beefsteak tomatoes looked juicy enough to eat off the vine.

After a tour of the garden, we'd have a lively conversation about the books she had been "reading" on tape and the new pictures sitting on her side tables next to her couch. I asked her what books she had read, she said that a couple of books had temporarily held her attention, yet she hadn't finished them. She'd ask me if I was working on any new books. Then she pointed to a picture of two women in jeans. Rather than make assumptions, I asked who was in the picture. She proudly said that it was a friend, and her sporting her first pair of jeans at the age of ninety. I admired her willingness to try new fashion, and after we all shared a laugh, Aunt Gail said she was ready to join us for lunch with martinis at her favorite restaurant.

A couple of years later, we visited Aunt Gail, again, joining her for lunch in the downstairs room. She had moved into a more advanced care unit. We were told that she had been having increasing memory problems, and we had not made plans to eat out. After our conversation with her downstairs, we moved to the comfort of her apartment. Her sense of humor was still evident since experiencing memory loss. She held my arm and looked at me as she explained, "I forget many things. They tell me that I repeat things sometimes, but if I don't care, then it doesn't matter." We both laughed and continued walking to her apartment.

As I reflect on my relationships with Grandma Trini and Aunt Gail and what they mean to me, I fully appreciate the wisdom, grace and resilience of these two women, and their impact on me. How these women cared for others and themselves exemplified the joy they imparted to those around them in their older years. In this way, they inspired me. I admired their willingness to change along with their changing needs as well as their interest in learning and trying new things, from moving to a new country to wearing the latest fashions. I've since learned about the different ways that older adults need and receive care. I know that older people close to us need different levels of care at different times. Both of these towering women in my life had families that provided the needed care as it became necessary.

Not all older people are fortunate enough or have access to the care they need. Of the topics that these seniors in this book talked about, the most critical issues were those of caregiving and financial security. Some of the most important relationships that seniors have is with those related to their healthcare. Older adults who have family members to care for them or who have the means to hire in-home care obviously have an advantage. At their best, those relationships can be supportive for both the senior and caregiver. Even through the stressors of these close caregiving situations, the relationship between the caregiver and the senior can mitigate the negative effects o health problems and needs.[2]

In the United States, aging is a social justice issue. The social justice ideal would make the proper care of housing and caregiving available to every older adult. The American Society on Aging proposes some ways on how to advance justice in aging, particularly concerning healthcare and housing[3]

To help seniors age at home, as many prefer to do, and to remain in their communities would require Congress to reauthorize the Older Americans Act. The OAA, which provides a structure and funding for critical services that older adults rely upon to remain independent, healthy, and connected to their families and communities. The services provide meals, benefits counseling, caregiver support, transportation, health promotion, legal services and more. These are all key to alleviating poverty and, when combined with effective Medicaid programs, to keeping elders from being institutionalized unnecessarily.[4]

Equally critical is the alleviation of the economic stresses of many seniors, which the Justice in Aging (JIA), the national non-profit legal advocacy organization proposes. When fiscal scarcity isolates those seniors immobilized by poverty, their social connections and this critical relationship are hindered.

Most older adults rely primarily on Social Security, resulting in financial insecurity. The American Society on Aging proposes that seniors with limited sources of income need to have an improved Supplemental Security Income (SSI) program. These benefits have not been updated since SSI's inception in 1972.[5] Originally, the Supplemental Security Income Restoration Act was intended to assist those with financial constraints as well as people in poverty.

Access to adequate health care is urgent for many older adults who live in food deserts, medical deserts, or find themselves alone. In situations where medical specialists are unavailable in nearby communities, social justice policy would, theoretically call for programs to provide adequate care and housing.

Presently, like no recent time has the US population been in the collective fear and distress that became apparent in early 2020. The Center for Disease Control announced a pandemic of the coronavirus, COVID-19, that could be contracted by all age groups. Seniors sixty years of age and older were the most in danger of the life-threatening symptoms of the virus.

Coronavirus claimed thousands of lives in China and Europe by the time it arrived in the US. Although the virus knows no borders, age group, or ethnic identity, seniors and people with preexisting health conditions have the highest death rates and remain the most vulnerable in this pandemic.

To prevent the spread of the virus, the CDC recommended that everyone practice physical distancing. Some states immediately mandated that people remain six feet from anyone around them outside their homes. In some states, people were instructed to stay in their homes unless they worked in essential services such as health care, food services, and transportation. Stores remaining open understood the imperative to protect everyone's health. To protect seniors, the stores gave seniors priority to shop during the first hour the stores opened. The health of older adults was taken seriously. They were allowed to shop for groceries for one hour before stores opened to the general public. Protective measures to wear masks and remain six feet apart held for workers and shoppers.

In communities where people sheltered at home, the policy included seniors living alone. They were allowed to have a caregiver or family member visit them. From the initial stages of this outbreak in the US, seniors living in nursing homes and other senior facilities closed to visitors. Although the mandate intended to prevent further spread of the virus, seniors in these facilities are often the ones in great need of a social connection with loved ones. Many in this age group do not have the technology or the skill necessary to reach out to others, which would prevent feelings of isolation.

Almost overnight, loneliness was the least of their concern. Some nursing homes that did not have protection for their workers began reporting a rapid increase in patients seriously ill from the coronavirus.

Before long, there was a sharp spike in deaths reported from those facilities. Claims that the outbreaks occurred due to unprotected healthcare providers led authorities to take action and close some facilities. The need to support all generations as it pertains to senior welfare has never been as clear. Younger age groups may be the caregivers, and others may be family members in family homes and need full support to maintain healthy environments, where they live as part of an extended family. Responsible senior residences quickly began to implement safety regulations to protect not only the seniors but the staff in those facilities.

As of this writing, the uncertainty of the length of time that the social distancing and shelter at home regulations will remain in place. Every day feels feel like an eternity for the unprotected populations. Those already vulnerable due to poverty, inadequate healthcare, and housing, as in the Native Americans, Latinos, and African American communities, have been more severely impacted. Many in these groups live in crowded conditions and fail to receive appropriate healthcare even in the best of times. Healthcare, housing, and economic support systems of older adult populations calls for a major rehaul as we transverse the global coronavirus pandemic. A new vision for how to support the most vulnerable groups rests on all of us. We need to envision and fashion new inclusive network systems to provide for all populations during a crisis and consider the particular needs of the older group.

A great deal more needs to be learned about testing for the virus, the most effective treatments for the disease and a vaccine. It has taken a pandemic of this magnitude for the world to learn about the cracks in the systems. All generations are facing confusing and troubled times. The inequities of the educational system have yet to see the fallout. Young career people are deferring their dreams. Workers struggle to pay the rent and put food on the table while facing job insecurity. Businesses are forced to close as workers and materials become unavailable while other workers risk their lives to provide healthcare and goods for everyone else. However, before us rests the golden opportunity that cannot be ignored to develop public policies to protect the older adults and the most vulnerable in society.

At this time, the country and the world are only at the beginning stages of this global crisis. History remains to be written on the impact that the pandemic is creating in the scientific, social, economic, and political arenas. There is enormous uncertainty for how the US and the global community will reorganize the economic and other systems that have been strained dramatically by the coronavirus. After record-high unemployment and long lines waiting for a bag of food, the businesses and workers will phase into some degree of operation. As the public ventures from their protected shelters, the hope is that the safety nets for workers in all industries and businesses will be incorporated into the overhaul for a more equitable, humane, and just society.

I end *Wings of a Firebird,* remembering the stories in this book and some of the wisdom people shared as they navigated difficult times. Presently many feel isolated during the pandemic and the mandated separation from others. The storytellers in this book found that the strength in their experiences from connections with family and social networks were paramount. They learned social distancing does not mean emotional distancing. During this time, when life is in turmoil, eliminating false borders that separate us and prevent real collective action is needed. In the folk story, the Firebird led the people in despair to safety. At this time, many are looking for the Firebird to find the way to safety. Until then, society has a great deal of work ahead caring for everyone, especially the most vulnerable. Meeting the complex needs of the broader diverse, aging population in this society requires expertise from every sector of the workforce.

ACKNOWLEDGMENTS

As with all of my previous books, I'm reminded of a salient realization-that as solitary as my work sometimes feels, I don't work alone. My storytelling depends on a community of people along with those whose stories are featured in my books.

I sincerely thank all of the interviewees who contributed to shaping the bigger story of relationships in our adult lives. The names are many and I deeply appreciate everyone for sharing your important relationships and amazing lives, including your joys, fears, loves, doubts, tragedies, and surprises in this period of your life. By the time I finished writing the book, these people felt like part of my family. They shortened the distance between us and surrounded me like a warm caress. I experienced a new clarity, and even at times epiphanies about aging.

I'm honored to be able to share the stories of loved ones who have left their life lessons for us to tell: my father Juan, Maria my mother, my grandmother Trini and grandfather Demetrio, my father-in-law Richard Baxter Thompson, and Aunt Gail Hanson. Their lives cut across many borders as revealed in this book.

A few collaborators contributed in indispensable ways.

First, I'm grateful to my husband, Dudley. Your skillful editing, design expertise, support, and loving interest in my creative endeavors makes it all more meaningful.

To Debra Ratner, gifted writer, tough editor, and committed mentor, I always appreciate your selfless knowledge and deftness that inspires me to stretch beyond a comfort zone.

Luz Guerra is a new connection for me. I was excited for the opportunity to work with you-a social justice warrior writer. I learned a great deal from your progressive insights that deepened my work.

I've been fortunate to live near a colleague and friend Jon Wagner. I'm glad for the proximity that makes our coffee and lunch meetings possible. Even during the pandemic our conversations about mutual interests of Anthropology continued on Face Time and internet. Thank you for keeping me focused and re-envisioning parts of this book.

It's always a treat to work with David Quijada, friend and collaborator. Our discussions on shared interests help to shape my ideas of community in my writing.

To my dear friend Beverly Elkan, I'm saddened that you won't be here to read my published book since our rich conversations helped me to see myself in this story of aging. Our talks about writing and storytelling went silent too soon, but your humor and wisdom continue to inspire me.

Last but by no means least, I am especially grateful to Claire Voet and Laura Redmond of Blossom Spring Publishing for your professional support and care in the publishing of my book. It's been a pleasure working with you.

SOURCES

Endnote

Introduction

1   The people in this book toured me through their lives in relationships with family, friends, and various social networks, relating how those relationships change over time. Work, money, health, spirituality, and wisdom impact most relationships. These matters become challenges in later years. Through the prism of these issues older adults can understand their differences and commonalities.

     I collected stories of older adults through personal visits, phone conferences, and Skyping. Some did not have access to computers, making long distance phone conversations the best option. A few preferred phone connections as a way to have some distance in order to talk about personal feelings. In general, interviews quickly became longer than casual conversations and were substantially rich with emotion and insight.

     Speaking intimately about their lives felt more comfortable for some participants than others. That is, talking with me about their life story was not a problem. However, some storytellers requested that their names remain anonymous. I honored their request and decided to assign all participants a first name pseudonym for the sake of consistency.

     I edited the interviews to make a readable story while maintaining people's authentic voices. Parts of some of the original interviews were omitted to keep their story and the theme fluid these are noted by ellipsis.

Every interview was at least a couple of hours long, but when compiling the book, it was necessary to include only the parts of the interviewees' stories that fit themes of particular chapters.

1

A New Day

1   Kottler, Jeffrey A., Jon Carlson, Bradford Keeney (2004) American Shaman: An Odyssey of Global Healing Traditions. NY, New York: Routledge Press.

2   Arrien, Angeles (2005).
The Second Half of Life. Boulder: Sounds True Inc.
Carlson, Jon (2004). *American Shaman: The Odyssey of Global Healing Traditions.* Routledge: New York: NY. Pp158.

3   Whitfield, Charles (1987). *Healing the Child Within.* Health Communications Inc. Deerfield Beach, Florida.

4   Roberto, Karen, A. (2015). Abusive Relationships in Late Life. In Kenneth Ferraro and Linda George (Eds.) *Handbook on Aging and Social Sciences, 8th Edition.* Academic Press: Cambridge, MA.,pp. 337-351. Bows, Hannah. 2019. *Violence Against Older Women, Volume II.* Hampshire, England. Palgrave Macmillan. Dunlop, Burton D., Beaulaurier, Richard, L. Seff, Laura R., Nena Newman, Malik, /fyster, Molissa. (2005).Domestic Violence Against Older Women: final Technical Report. Washington, DC: *Research Report Submitted to US Dept. of Justice.*

5   The National Domestic Violence Hotline, 2014
     "Get the Facts & Figures,"
     https://www.thehotline.org/resources/statistics/.

6   Pan, Amy, and Sandra Daley, Lourdes M. Rivera,
     Kara Williams, Danielle Lingle, Vivian Reznik. 2006.
     "Understanding the role of culture in domestic
     violence." The Ahimsa Project for Safe Families.
     Journal of Immigrant and Minority Health 8 (1), 35-
     43. Carr, Deborah.   (2004). Gender, pre loss
     marital dependence, and older adults' adjustment
     to widowhood. *Journal of Marriage and Family*,
     66:220–235.

     Fisher, Bonnie. S and Therese Zink, Saundra L.
     Regan. 2011. "Abuses against older women:
     Prevalence and health effects." *Journal of
     Interpersonal Violence, 26*(2): 254–268.

7   Beaulaurier, Richard, Seff, Laura, and Newman,
     Frederick L. 2008. "Barriers to Help-Seeking for
     Older Women Who Experience Intimate Partner
     Violence: A Descriptive Model." *Journal of
     Women and Aging* 20 (3): 231-248.

     Brownell, Patricia. 2016.   Older Women and
     Intimate Partner Violence. *The Encyclopedia of
     Adulthood and Aging*, First Edition.   Edited by
     Susan Krauss Whitbourne. John Wiley & Sons,
     Inc. 1-5.

8   Umberson, Debra., & Jennifer Montez. 2010.
     "Social Relationships and Health: A Flashpoint
     for Health Policy." *Journal of Health and Social
     Behavior*, 51. 54-66.

9   Ibid. 2011. Fisher, Bonnie and Therese Zink Saundra L. Regan. 254–268. National Coalition Against Domestic Violence   NCADV. 2012. https://www.speakcdn.com/assets/2497/domestic_violence2.pdf

National Coalition Against Domestic Violence. 2018. https://ncadv.org/statistics.

Brooks, Kathleen. 2012.. *Radical Integrity: Ways to Heal Your Inner Child and Create a True Adult.* San Diego: EthicaLife Press.

Schacter-Shalomi, Zalman and Ronald S. Miller. 1995. *From Age-Ing to Sage-Ing: A Profound New Vision of Growing Older.* New York: Grand Central Publishing.

Richmond, Lewis. 2012. *Aging as a Spiritual Practice.* New York: Gotham Books.

Nhat Hanh, Thich, 2006. *Reconciliation: Healing the Inner Child.* Berkeley: Parallax Press.

2

<u>Someone to Care for Me</u>

1   Saulsby, Laura and Kate Bennet. 2015. "How Relationships Help Us to Age Well." *The Psychologist* 28 (2): 110-113.

Abbit, Linda. 2017. *The Conscious Caregiver: A Mindful Approach to Caring for Your Loved One Without Losing Yourself.* New York: Adams Media Imprint of Simon & Schuster.

Beard, John R. and Simon Biggs, David E. Bloom, Linda P. Fried, Paul Hogan, Alexandre Kalache, S. Jay Olshansky, eds., 2011. *Global Population Ageing: Peril or Promise.* Geneva: World Economic Forum: 57-60.

2   Hansson, Isabelle, Buratti, Sandra, Thorvaldsson, Valgier, Johansson, Boo, and Berg, Anne Ingeborg October 2017. "Changes in Life Satisfaction in the Retirement Transition: Interaction Effects of Transition Type and Individual Resources." *Work, Aging and Retirement.* Volume (4): 352-366.

3   Cornwell, Benjamin., Laurmann, Edward O. & Chumm, L.Phillip. 2008. "The Social connectedness of Older Adults." *American Sociological Review* 73 (2): 185-203.

4   Becerra, Rosina M. 1983. "The Mexican American Aging in a Changing Culture" in *Aging in Minority Groups*. Beverly edited by R.L. McNeely and J. L. Colen, 108-118. Hills: Sage Publications.

5   Hayes-Bautista, David E., Werner O. Schink, and Jorge Chapa. 1990. *The Burden of Support: Young Latinos in an Aging Society*. Stanford: Stanford University Press.

Hyunsook, Yoon and Jon Hendricks 2018. *Handbook of Asian Aging*. New York: Taylor & Francis Group, 391.

3

Trusting New Realities

1   Connidis IA, McMullin J. Ambivalence. 2002. "Family Ties and Doing Sociology." *Journal of Marriage and Family*. (64): 594–601.

Bengtson, Vern L, Biblarz, Timothy J, Roberts, Robert E. L. 2002. *How Families Still Matter: A Longitudinal Study of Youth in Two Generations.* Cambridge University Press; New York.

2   Luescher, Kurt and Karl Pillemer. 1998. "Intergenerational Ambivalence: A New Approach to the Study of Parent-Child Relations in Later Life. "*Journal of Marriage and the Family* 60 (2): 413-425.

3   Ashrafzadeh, Sahar, 2017. "Medical Deserts in America: Why we Need to Advocate for Rural Healthcare." (blog). Harvard Global Health Institute. https://globalhealth.harvard.edu/blog/medical-deserts-america-why-we-need-advocate-rural-healthcare

National Rural Health Association, 2019. NRHA Save Rural Hospitals Action Center. https://www.ruralhealthweb.org/advocate/save-rural-hospitals.

4   Ostroff, Caitlin and Bri'd Frisbie, Ciara. 2017. "Millions of Americans live nowhere near a hospital, jeopardizing their lives." CNN analysis

of data from Centers for Medicare and Medicaid Services, https://www.cnn.com/2017/08/03/health/hospital-deserts/index.html.

5   Darden, Antonia 1995. *Culture and Difference: Critical Perspectives on the Bicultural Experience in the United States.* Bergin and Garvey: Westport, Connecticut.

Calzada, Esther J., Fernandez, Yenny, and Cortes, Dharna E. 2010. "Incorporating the Cultural Value of Respeto into a Framework of Latino Parenting." *Cultural Diversity Ethnic Minority Psychology.* January 16 (1):77-86.

6   Angeles Arrien 2005. *The Second Half of Life: Opening the Eight Gates of Wisdom.* Sounds True, Inc. Boulder, CO.

7   Ibid. Darden, 1995.

8   Martinez, Mario. 2017. *The MindBody Self: How Longevity is Culturally Learned and the Causes of Health are Inherited.* Hay House: Carlsbad, CA

9   Bengtson, Vern L, Giarrusso, Roseann, Mabry, J. Beth and Silverstein, Merril. 2002. "Solidarity, Conflict, and Ambivalence: Complementary or Competing Perspectives on Intergenerational Relationships?" *Journal of Marriage and Family*; (64): 568–576.

10 Connidis, Ingrid Arnet and Amanda Barnett, E. 2019. *Family Ties and Aging.* Thousand Oaks: Sage Publications.

11 Langner, Laura A. and Frank F Furstenberg. 2018. "Gender Differences in Spousal Caregivers' Care and Houework: Fact or Fiction?" *Journal of Gerontology* Series B., https://doi.org/10.1093/geronb/gbyo87.

12 Mitchell, Judith M and Bryan J. Kemp, 2000. "Quality of Life in Assisted Living Homes: A Multidimensional Analysis." *The Journals of Gerontology: Series B* 55 (2): 117-127.

    Bell, Mary, J. and Frank Whittington, Molly L. Perkins, Vickie Patterson, Carole V Hollingsworth, Sharon L King. Bess Combs. 2000. "Quality of Life in Assisted Living Facilities: Viewpoints of Residents." *Journal of Applied Gerontology* 19: (10): 304-325.

13 Ahrons, Constance R. 2007." Family Ties After Divorce: Long-Term Implications for Children." *Wiley Online Library* 4 (1): 53-65. https://onlinelibrary.wiley.com/doi/abs/10.1111/j.1545-5300.2006.00191.x.

    Queen, Joe 2018. Neuro-Logic: How Your Brain is Keeping You From Changing Your Mind. *The Rotarian.* 38-43.

4

In Service of Others

1   Jungsu Ryu & Jinmoo Heo. 2015. "Relationships between leisure activity types and well-being in older adults." *Journal of Activities, Adaptation, and Aging* 39 (1): 331-342.

Chang Po-Ju, Linda Wray, and Yeqiang Lin. 2017, March 17/18. "Social Relationships, Leisure Activity, and Health in Older Adults." *Health Psychology* 33. (6): 516-523.

2   Mejia, Mercedes. 2017, July 10th. "Anishinaabe Water Walkers Trek from Minnesota to Quebec to Honor Great Lakes"-BBC World Service. http://michiganradio.org/post/anishinaabe-water-walkers-trek-minnesota-quebec-honor-great-lakes

3   Freedman, Marc. 2002. "Civic windfall? Realizing the promise in an aging America." *Generations,* 26: (2), 86-89.

Morrow-Howell, Nancy, Jim Hinterlong, Philip A. Rozarios & Fengyan Tang. 2003. "Effects of Volunteering and the well-being of older adults". *Journal of Gerontology* (2):137-145.

Torres-Gil, Fernando. 2014. "Aging in a Majority-Minority Nation." In (editor) Paul H. Irving with Rita Beamish. *The Upside of Aging: How Long Life is Changing the World of Health,*

Work, Innovation, Policy and Purpose. NJ: Wiley and Sons: Hoboken. Pp. 179-194.

4   Sezaki, Shinya and Bloomgarden, Joan. 2000: "Home-based Art Therapy for Older Adults." *Journal of the American Art Therapy Association* 17: (4): 283-90.

5   Bayer, Steven. 2002. *Tikkum Olam: To Speak on Behalf of the World.*   Brooklyn, NY: KTAV Publishing House.

PART 2

5

A Dollar Away

1   Rupp, Kalman and Alexander Strand, Paul S. Davies. 2003. "Poverty Among Elderly Women: Assessing SSI Options to Strengthen Social Security Reform." *The Journals of Gerontology* 58: (6): 359-368.

2   Butas, Marius., 2017. 6 Common Causes of Poverty in Aging Adults. Home Care Assistnce. (July 3) https://www.homecareassistancemesa.com/causes-of-poverty-in-seniors/.

3   Toossi, Mitra and Elka Torpey. 2017. "Older Workers: Labor Force Trends and Career Options." *Career Outlook.* Bureau of Labor Statistics.(May).https://www.bls.gov/careeroutlook/2017/article/older-workers.htm

     Brand, Jennie E. 2015. "The Far-Reaching Impact of Job Loss and Unemployment." *Annual Review of Sociology* 41. 359-375.

4   Ibid. Rupp. 2003.
     Fisher, Jonathan D. David S. Johnson, Marchand, Joseph T., Smeeding, Timothy M., Torrey, Barbara B. 2009." Identifying the Poorest Older

Americans." *The Journals of Gerontology 64* (6): 758-766.

Ethan, Jack. 2012. Ageing and Financial (In) Security. In John R. Beard, Simon Biggs, David E. Bloom, Linda P. Fried, Paul Hogan, Alexandre Kalache, and S. Jay Olshansky, eds., *Global Population Ageing: Peril or Promise.* Geneva: World Economic Forum.

5   Munnell, Alicia H., Sanzenbacher, Geoffrey T., Rutledge, Matthew, S. 2015. "What Causes Workers to Retire Before They Plan?" (September). Research paper written for Center for Retirement Research at Boston College. http://crr.bc.edu/wp-content/uploads/2015/09/wp_2015-22.pdf.

6   Nelson, Todd, D. 2017. *Ageism: Stereotyping and Prejudice Against Older Persons-(*2nd Edition): Cambridge, Mass. MIT Press.

7   Kessler, Ronald C. and James S. House, J. Blake Turner. Unemployment and Health in a Community Sample. *Journal of Health and Social Behavior* 28 (1): 51-59.

Cubanski, Juliette, and Giselle Casillas, Anthony D'Amico. 2015. *Poverty Among Seniors: An Updated Analysis of National and State Level Poverty Rates Under the Official and Supplemental Poverty Measures.* Kaiser Family Foundation. (June) http://files.kff.org/attachment/issue-brief-poverty-among-seniors-an-updated-analysis-of-national-and-state-level-poverty-rates-under-the-official-and-supplemental-poverty-measures.

8   Thomas, Eugene, and L., McCabe, Esther, Berry, Jane E. 1980. "Unemployment and Family Stress: A Reassessment." *Family Relations*. The National Council on Family Relations 29 (4): 517-524.

9   United States Census on Poverty. 2018. Report by Jessica Semega, Melissa Kollar, John Creamer, And Abinash Mohanty. https://www.census.gov/content/dam/Census/library/publications/2019/demo/p60 266.pdf.

10   Peterson, Peter G, 1999. "Gray Dawn: The Global Aging Crisis." *Foreign Affairs* (1): 42-55.

Chavez, Koji, Christopher Wimer, and David Betson. 2015. "Medical Needs and Poverty Among the Elderly Population: The Role of Out-Of-Pocket Medical Expenditures and Assets under the Supplemental Poverty Measure." Working Paper. Stanford, CA: Stanford Center on Poverty and Inequality.

6

<u>The Grace of Showing Up</u>

1   Silverstein, Merril, Lendon, Jessica, and Giarruso, Roseann (2012). Ethnic & Cultural Diversity in Aging Families: Implications for Resource Allocation and Well Being & Cross Generations in Rosemary Bliensner's (edited volume), *Handbook of Families and Aging (2nd Edition)*. Westport: Prager. Pp: 287-308.

Everard, Kelly M. and Helen W. Lach, Edwin B. Fisher, Carolyn M Baum 2000. Relationship of Activity and Social Support to the Functional Health of Older Adults. *The Journals of Gerontology: Series B.* 55. (4), 208-212.

2   United States Census Bureau (November, 2018). Families and Living Arrangements.

3   Bahrampour, Tara. 2013. "As families change, grandparents are stepping in to take care of grandchildren" (November, 5): *Washington Post*.

Cox, Carole B. 2010. "Policy and Custodial Grandparents." *Marquette Elder's Advisor 11.* (2): 281-30.

4   Ibid: Cox. 2010. 281-305.

5   Esme Fuller-Thomson, PhD, Meredith Minkler, Dr PH, and Diane Driver, PhD. 1997. A Profile

of Grandparents Raising Grandchildren In The United States. The Gerontological Society of America. *The Gerontologist* 37. (3): 406-4.

Senior Economic Security Symposium, 2013, Preparing Older Adults and Communities for a New Economic Reality. *Center for Retirement Research at Boston College*: www.friendshipcenters.org.

7   Cox, Carole B. 2000. Why Grandchildren are Going to and Staying at Grandmother's House and What Happens When They Get There, In To Grandmother's House We Go and Stay. Perspectives on Custodial Grandparents 3. *International Sociology* 24. (3): 5-345.

Cruikshank, Margaret (2013). *Learning to Be Old: Gender, Culture, and Aging.* Rowman & Littlefield Publishes, Inc. Boulder.

8   Goodwin, James and Diana Miller. 2017. *Interview on "Building Age Friendly Cities for Elders.* Forum Radio Program KQED. (July 26th).

PART 3

7

<u>Alchemy</u>

1   Chum, Bun Lam and Susan M. McHale, Kimberly A. Updegraff. 2012. Gender dynamics in Mexican American families: Connecting mothers', fathers', and youths' experiences. *Sex Roles* 67. (1-2).17-28.

2   Radina, Elise, M. 2007. "Mexican American Siblings Caring for aging parents: Processes of caregiver selection/designation." *Journal of Comparative Family Studies* 38, (1)143-168.

3   Borgas, George. 2007. *Mexican Immigration to the United States National Bureau of Economic Research Conference Report- 2ⁿᵈ edition."* Chicago, Ill: University of Chicago Press.

    Hirschman, Charles, 2013. "The contribution of Immigrants to American Culture. "*Daedalus*, 142 (3). 10:1162.

4   Waters, Mary C. and Marisa Gerstein. (Eds.). 2015. "The Integration of Immigrants Into American Society." Washington, D.C: *National Academies of Sciences, Engineering and Medicine.*

Becerra, Rosina, M. 1983. "The Mexican-American: Aging in a Changing Culture" in *Aging in Minority Groups*, edited by R. L. McNeely, and, John, L, Colen 108-117. Beverly Hills: Sage Publications.

PART 1V

8

Reflections

1   Cornwell, B., Laurmann, E.O. & Chumm, L.P. 2008. "The Social Connectedness of Older Adults." *American Sociological Review*, 73, 185-203.

Cozolino, Luis, 2012. *The Neuroscience of Human Relations. 2nd Edition, Attachment and the Developing Social Brain*, WW Norton & Company, New York.

2   Ibid Rowe & Kahn. 1997.

Kohli, Martin. 2006. "Aging and Justice." *Handbook of Aging and the Social Sciences,* Sixth Edition. Academic Press: Cambridge, MA. 456-478.Soulsby, Laura and Kate Bennett. 2015. How Relationships Help Us to Age Well. *The Psychologist* 28. (2): 110-113.

Sokolovsky, Joy. 2009. "The Quest for Gerontopia: Culture and Health in Late Life" in *Cultural Context of Aging in World Wide Perspectives*, edited by Jay 491-498. Santa Barbara: CA.

3   Prindiville, Kevin 2019. "A Sweeping Vision for Justice in Aging." *Aging Today.* [May 1].

https://www.asaging.org/blog/sweeping-vision-justice-aging.

Chang, Po-Ju, Linda Wray, and Lin Yeqiang. 2014. "Social Relationships, Leisure Activity, and Health in Older Adults." *Health Psychology.* 2014 Jun; 33 (6): 516–523.

4   Rowe, John and Robert Kahn, R. 1997.
"Successful Aging." *The Gerontologist,* 37 (4):433-440.Watt, Richard G, and Anja Heilmann, Wael Sabbah, Tim Newton, Tarani Chandola, Jun Aida, Aubrey Sheiham, Michael Marmot, Ichiro Kawachi, Georgios Tsakos, 2014. "Social relationships and health related behaviors among older US adults." *Biomed Public Health 14 (*533): 1-11.
http://www.biomedcentral.com/1471-2458/14/533

5.   Ibid. Prindiville. 2019. (May 1).

Read about the author of this book Concha Delgado Gaitan, Ph. D.
https://www.blossomspringpublishing.com/team/concha-delgado-gaitan/

www.blossomspringpublishing.com

Made in the USA
Monee, IL
27 July 2020